The Great Sign

Messages and Visions of Final Warnings

Volume II

The Great Sign

Messages and Visions of Final Warnings

Volume II

by: Sadie Jaramillo

× J. M. J.
God Bless You!
Sadie

Bishop Roman Danylak
Titular Bishop of Nyssa
Church of Ss. Sergius and Bacchus
Piazza Madonna dei Monti, 3
00184 Roma

She approached me after Mass in the Church of Saint Sebastian in Garabandal. It was May 13, 1999, Feast and anniversary of the apparition of the Blessed Virgin in Fatima. It was the feast of the Ascension of Our Lord to heaven. She approached me with the words: 'Father Bishop, I come to convey to you the best wishes of Bishop Basil Filevich of Saskatoon, Canada. She couldn't have come with a better introduction. I had never heard of Sadie Jaramillo; but as I came to know the great deeds of Our Lord in her life over the following days, and to understand the predilection of the Blessed Virgin for this unassuming woman, I was overwhelmed by the story of the workings of God's grace in the life of this humble but precious flower of the love of Christ. Hers is the story of the miracles of divine love, of the grace and truth that came by Jesus Christ, in the heart and soul of one who hungers and thirsts for Him. The vesper prayers for the Feast of the Sacred Heart of Jesus according to the Byzantine Ukrainian rite, present the beggar Canaanite woman who came to plead for her daughter.. " Most merciful Jesus, how could Your heart have closed itself before the pleas of the unfortunate Canaanite woman, who cried after You and pleaded, 'Have compassion on me, O Lord, Son of David. My daughter suffers grievously in the clutches of the demons.' And You did not reply one word to her please, and even as she fell to her knees, You humbled her: 'It is not right to give the bread of the children to throw it to the dogs.' Where, O Lord is Your love for the unfortunate? And the prayers continue: 'I did not close my heart to the unfortunate. It beat with love for her; I showed this apparent harshness to manifest to the world her great virtue.' And she replied humbly. 'Yes, Lord but even the pups eat from the crumbs that fall from the table of their masters'. 'I could not hold back the love of my heart for her, and I cried out. 'Woman, great is your faith. May it be done according to your desires." The Lord not only received Sadie's contrite heart, her tears of sorrow, to wash her soul in His precious blood. He restored to her all she had lost and made her His voice to this unbelieving generation. I recommend to everyone these messages of Divine Mercy, and of the love of the Mother of our Salvation. Such is the love of Christ the Redeemeer.

Dated at Rome this 11th day of June, 1999
Feast of the Sacred Heart of Jesus

+ Roman Danylak,
Titular bishop Nyssa

Contents

Dedication .... *viii*
Declaration .... *ix*
Acknowledgements .... *x*
Foreword .... *xi*
Introduction .... *xiii*

Reconciliation! Conversion! Consecration! 1

Persecution Is Soon Upon Humanity 5

Many Will Receive Graces 9

My Children, Prepare For What Comes 20

A Great Outpouring Of My Spirit 25

My People Perish For Lack Of Knowledge 31

I Will Lead! I Will Gather! I Will Protect! 45

Woe To The Hardened Of Heart! 51

Visions 56

The Fire Of My Love! The Fire of My Justice!
The Fire Of My Purification 61

God's Great Prodigy Of Love 66

The Fulfillment Of Calvary Comes to Humanity! 75

Behold The Time Draws Near 81

Be Not Afraid! 91

All Will Know the Eucharistic Lord 103

Dedication

This work is dedicated to Our Lady of Sorrows, Maria – Virgin Pura and to Jesus Christ – King of All nations! May the Reign of Their Two Hearts descend soon into the hearts and minds of all mankind upon all the earth. Today Sadie Jaramillo is living that dedication as director of "The Father's House of Victory Through the Holy Family" apostolate in Santa Maria, California. At the Blessed Mother's direction this apostolate was founded to form the beginning of many prayer communities to receive and to teach the many who will come to take refuge in her serene valley of Santa Maria, under the "Cross of Peace," which she has asked to be built there. On September 23, 1997, the Blessed Mother promised: "The blessings upon all who participate and who in any way help bring this about will come through a special grace of protection for the coming days; and let all who would participate do so for the greater Glory of God!" For further information contact:

The Father's House of Victory Through the Holy Family
401 Garnet Way, Santa Maria, CA 93454, 805/928-3994

This book may not be reproduced in whole or in part by any means without the prior written permission of the publisher.

The publisher reserves all copyrights, but encourages everyone to read and distribute these messages, so that all people may become aware of these last days and reconcile themselves to Our Lord and Savior Jesus Christ – King of All Nations!

Copyright© 2000 Signs of the Times Apostolate, Inc.

ISBN: 1-892165-03-1

All Rights Reserved.

Published by: St. Dominic's Media   Phone 703-327-2277
               P.O. Box 345   FAX 703-327-2888
               Herndon, VA 20172-0345   www.sign.org

Declaration

Since the abolition of Canons 1399 and 2318 of the former Code of Canon Law, publications about new appearances, revelations, prophecies, miracles, etc., may be distributed and read by the faithful without the express permission of the Church, providing they contain nothing which contravenes faith and morals. This means no imprimatur is necessary when distributing information on new apparitions not yet judged by the Church.

In Lumen Gentium, Vatican II, Chapter 12, the Council Fathers instructed the faithful:

"That discernment in matters of faith is aroused and sustained by the Spirit of truth. It is exercised under the guidance of the sacred teaching authority, in faithful and respectful obedience to which the people of God accepts that which is not just the word of men but truly the word of God. (Cf. 1 Thess. 2:13).
Through it, the people of God adheres unwaveringly to the faith given once and for all to the saints, (Cf. Jud. 3) penetrates it more deeply with right thinking, and applies it more fully in its life.

It is not only through the sacraments and the ministries of the Church that the Holy Spirit sanctifies and leads the people of God and enriches it with virtues, but, 'allotting his gifts to everyone according as He wills.' (1 Cor. 12:11) He distributes special graces among the faithful of every rank. By these gifts He makes them fit and ready to undertake the various tasks and offices which contribute toward the renewal and building up of the Church, according to the words of the Apostle: 'The manifestation of the Spirit is given to everyone for profit.' (1 Cor. 12:7). These charisms, whether they be the more outstanding or the more simple and widely diffused, are to be received with thanksgiving and consolation for they are perfectly suited to and useful for the needs of the Church. Extraordinary gifts are not to be sought after, nor are the fruits of the apostolic labor to be presumptuously expected from their use; but judgement as to their genuinity and proper use belongs to those who are appointed leaders in the Church, to whose special competence it belongs, not indeed to extinguish the Spirit, but to test all things and hold fast to that which is good." (Cf 1 Thess. 5:12, 19-21).

All of the messages contained in this volume have been reviewed by two Catholic priests: Fr. John B. Wang, Ph.D., J.U.D., and Fr. James W. Anderson, M.S.A., J.D., Ph.D., who find nothing in them to be contrary to faith or morals. Nevertheless, both Sadie Jaramillo and the publishers of this supplement to The Great Sign unconditionally submit them to the final and official judgment of the Magisterium of the Church.

Acknowledgments

We wish to acknowledge and thank those who have helped prepare this book for publication. Many thanks to Fr. John Wang and Fr. Jim Anderson for critically reviewing all the messages prior to this publication, and to Darlene and Mel Cassio for typing them and preparing the manuscript for publication.

Most especially we give thanks to God Our loving Father for sending His Son, The Holy Spirit, and our Blessed Mother to speak to our hearts.

Foreword

This second volume of visions and explanations given by Heaven to Sadie Jaramillo provides timely insight and hope to those seeking to make sense out of a world spinning wildly out of control. These visions and explanations are not catalogues of divine threats. Rather, they are initiatives of love to us from each divine person of the Blessed Trinity, and from our Holy Mother, Mary. Although Sadie stopped receiving messages, as such, in the spring of 1998, she continues to receive visions which are later explained to her. Reading them reminds one of the visions given to the prophet Ezekiel, and to St. John in his Apocalypse, and motivates one to read, pray and meditate on their visions again.

In the visions and explanations to Sadie, Heaven is telling us clearly that our problem is neglect, even outright rejection of God, and nearly total self-indulgence, resulting in promiscuity, abortion and other forms of murder and violence, greed, hatred, intolerance, indifference, and on and on. St. Paul expresses it clearly in Galatians, Chapter 5. If Jesus' Church would lead us firmly to leave these behind, and to live joyfully in the Holy Spirit, His fruits of love, joy, peace, patience, kindness, goodness, trustfulness, gentleness and self-control would prevail. Then the people would reject world leaders who lie, murder, betray, and lead their people to sin and war. Then the triumph of God's Church would come without tribulation and chastisement. Hosea 14:2

Early in January 1999, our Beloved Father told Sadie that the world would pass through a trial by fire: the fire of His mercy, justice, and purification. The fire of mercy refers to the warning, or illumination of souls. The fire of purification refers to God's cleansing of the earth of all that is evil in preparation for a coming Era of Peace. On January 26 the Holy Spirit asked Sadie to publicize His wish that the whole Church pray to Him for 30 days for a great harvest of souls following the warning.

In March 1999, Sadie was shown a white, a red, a black and a pale horse with riders. She was referred to Apocalypse, Chapter 6 for an explanation. She also saw 7 angels, each holding a bowl full of God's wrath. She was referred to Apocalypse 15:1-8 for an explanation. But she was also told that because many had prayed, the time of mercy had been extended, and the time of justice had been shortened. On May 21, 1999, while returning home from a pilgrimage to Garabandal, Jesus gave

Sadie an urgent message asking His people for prayer and for courage. "Tell my children: 'Do not fear!' I come swiftly to establish a new era, a new reign through my Eucharistic Heart and the Immaculate Heart of Mary, My Mother! Pray still for my brothers the priests! They do not know what awaits them."

I invite you to renew and refresh yourself in reading these visions and explanations from Heaven to Sadie, and to follow their plea to recommit yourself to prayer, fasting, adoration of the Blessed Sacrament, and to living totally in the Divine Will. Maranatha! Come, Lord Jesus Christ!

Fr. Jim Anderson, M.S.A.
Spiritual Director, The Father's House of Victory Through the Holy Family Apostolate

September 12, 1999
In honor of the Holy Name of Mary

Introduction

I have been asked in regard to the messages, "What do Our Lord and Our Lady want me to do to PREPARE spiritually?"

None of this makes any sense if you do not already know JESUS AND OUR LADY! You first of all need to INVITE THEM INTO YOUR HEART!!!

Recognize that your free will is what gets in GOD'S way! Abandon yourself to the Will of God the Father, as we say in THE OUR FATHER, "Thy Kingdom COME. Thy WILL BE DONE on earth AS IT IS IN HEAVEN."

Reconcile yourself to your God by returning to the sacraments. IF YOU ARE NOT IN A STATE OF GRACE, I IMPLORE YOU, DO NOT WAIT, GO TO CONFESSION, AND BE HEALED IN THAT GREAT SACRAMENT OF HEALING. Then Jesus, <u>who is really present in the EUCHARIST, can come into your heart and begin the life changing experience of walking and talking with you about everything in your life.</u>

The messages have not been given to put us into a spirit of fear, but rather, so that we can know the SIGNS OF THE TIMES which those around us, who are not praying and have not yet converted are blind to. But if you have begun this faith walk, then know that the promises of God are faithful, tried, and true. Our Lady will lead you and protect you. I have been given the understanding that everyone consecrated to The Two Hearts, AND LIVING THAT CONSECRATION, will be interiorly alerted to the coming events.

Another question I receive is, "What about material preparations?" Our Lord and Our Lady are not asking us to mortgage everything we own to buy material things. But as in the parable of the ten virgins, five went out and GOT THEIR OIL. This is symbolic of what we are to do, within our means! What Our Lord is looking for is an action of faith. The five virgins did something. THEY WENT OUT AND GOT THE OIL FOR THEIR LAMPS! It doesn't say they went out and bought premium oil, or low cost oil, it just says they did SOMETHING in faith, because they believed and they wanted to be ready. If you have been through a natural disaster, you know what will not be readily available. Not food because the markets are closed. Not water because of contamination or broken pipelines. Not cash because the ATMs are not working. Not gas because gas pumps operate on electricity. Pray before the Blessed Sacrament, and ask the Holy Spirit to guide you and tell you what to do. HE WILL.

Be prudent. Do what you can, and God will do the rest. But we ARE required to move in faith. An action is required. You would be PRESUMING on God if you said, "Well, I could do something, but God will take care of me." Yes, the time will come when we will see great miracles, and God will provide. But right now He wants to see us move in faith ACCORDING TO OUR MEANS, AND WHAT WE ARE ABLE TO DO!

If you can really do nothing because of unbelieving partners, financial status, etc., then yes, HE WILL take care of you. I believe that at some point things that are happening (events happening around the world, crisis, natural disaster, etc.) will convince our unbelievers and they will do in a little bit of time, what others have had a long time to do.

TRUST, TRUST, and TRUST. In the Message of March 20,

1997, Our Lord told me to look up the word TRUST and put HIS NAME, JESUS where the definition indicated.

TRUST: 1) Strong belief that someone (JESUS) can be depended on;
2) The one (JESUS) that is trusted;
3) Something that has been put in one's care (JESUS) or charge;
4) Rely, depend on (JESUS).

Ultimately, that is the only thing we have for the days ahead, OUR FAITH, AND TRUST IN THE PROMISES THAT OUR LORD AND OUR LADY HAVE MADE TO US.

The messages and visions included in this volume II of The Great Sign are those that have been received by me between March 25, 1998, and December 9, 1999.

Sadie Jaramillo

Reconciliation! Conversion! Consecration!

Message to Sadie Jaramillo – March 25, 1998, 5:00 a.m.

SJ: I heard a voice and I tested. Mary responded.

Mary: I am of God, I am She who conceived by the Power of the Spirit of God! From the Tabernacle of My womb, The Word Incarnate came into the world!

Write your visions:

SJ: In preparation for the Cross of Peace 10th Anniversary, members of the prayer group gathered with me for a novena. We entrusted this novena to Saint Joseph and Saint Michael.

Visions: For three of those nine days, while praying, I could see Our Lady of Guadalupe crying tears of blood. The last of the three days I saw Our Lady of Guadalupe with three swords with the points meeting over the top of Her gown where Her Heart would be. I clearly was given "abortion, homosexuality, sins of the flesh (impurity)."

During the two days of the anniversary, there were two more images of Our Lady crying tears. These were seen by many people.

Sunday night, I collapsed into bed, after the long weekend of speaking and praying with people. I was given the following vision: I was shown a coffin, and in the coffin was Our Holy Father, John Paul II. The coffin was open, and there were cardinals all around the coffin, talking and looking at him. There was definitely no sorrow.

Early the next morning, my spiritual director from Rome called and it was during his prayer for me that I was given the understanding these are they who plot the death of the Holy Father. A second time this vision was given with a significant difference. To the right side of the coffin is standing Our Lady and Saint Michael, and it seems they are holding satan at bay, for he is trying to reach the cardinals around the Holy Father.

Our Lady continues:

Mary: My little sorrowful rose, with great love I embrace all those who lovingly worked so tirelessly to minister to the thousands that come (to the Cross of Peace Tenth Anniversary). **I confirmed the message being given with the two images that wept tears! Reconciliation! Conversion! Consecration!**

The time left now is nearly expired. My children do you not understand? Though the warning of man's conscience was to have come long ago, this would certainly have meant that the length of time of the anti-christ's reign would have been longer! As it is now, I have shortened the length of his reign. Only by your continued prayers and sacrifices united and given to Me with love have I been able to intervene! (Do) **you understand My sorrow?**

Continued abortions, sexual perversion and that which I revealed at Fatima, sins of the flesh, cause more souls to go to hell!! (The three swords in the vision.)

You see now the beginning of the fulfillment of much revealed to you and others. The increase in loss of life in accidents, the destruction of homes during these storms, the shocking crimes being committed, all these are signs

for My children. Satan knows no limit to his fury against you My remnant! But I am faithful to My promises and nothing can happen lest it be permitted by God!

Thus you must now see His Divine Love in His Divine Will. Through your sorrows you imitate and are intimately united to Our Hearts, if you accept with Love your sorrows! Recall all that has been said. Look and see how I have sustained you up to now, and you will not fear what comes soon!

The time is now for the cross! The time is now for the cross! The time is now for the cross! As Moses was sent to Pharaoh to say, "Thus sayeth the Lord your God, let my people go," C., I tell you now is the time to go and ask for the land. I will send you two who will speak on behalf of My Project with you.

As the suffering of Carol's heart has been borne with great love and resignation to the Will of God, now too, the suffering in your heart must rest in the Will of God! If you feel at times you walk alone, I tell you again, you do not walk alone. My Son and I walk with you.

This humanity would self-destruct if it were not for Divine Intervention which will increasingly be evident as the days progress. Walk in faith. Believe in what you cannot yet see, for soon you will see it!

On this Feast of the Annunciation I gave My Fiat! Today give Me yours, and together We will Triumph! I encourage you with Love to embrace your suffering. A broken and humble spirit God will not turn away! He is your strength, your protection, your source of all good things, and this is what I obtain for you! When Gods appointed time comes, many things will happen, but I ask you to remember He is in control!

Blessings descend upon you and all who believe!

SJ: Amen.

Persecution Is Soon Upon Humanity

<u>Vision given to Sadie Jaramillo – April 26, 1998 – St. John the Evangelist Chapel, during rosary after mass.</u>

SJ: I see Jesus stooped down and he has drawn the Christian symbol of the fish on the ground. I can see this clearly. He then rises and calls me to follow Him. There are others standing, watching. It appears that they are the apostles. As I follow Jesus through a door, I am shown a scene where the Holy Father is walking the Via Dolorosa. He is carrying a cross and he looks as he looks now, frail and tired. It seems strange to me for the Via Dolorosa is in a coliseum. I can see people sitting and as the Holy Father continues to walk and I see in the faces of some in the crowd anger and hatred. The Holy Father then stops walking, but the cross does not fall from his shoulder. He then begins to read from a scroll made of parchment. My vision ends.

<u>Message to Sadie Jaramillo – April 28, 1998, 3:30 p.m.</u>

Mary: Have I not brought you here? Your Mother and the Mother of all humanity? I am She, who brought forth the Savior of the World from my womb, Flesh of my flesh, SAVIOR DIVINE! Oh child, my little sorrowful rose, how little time is left! I know your fatigue in this journey to bring the messages of hope and consolation, but many graces are being poured out upon my children! All has been prepared for you to journey as our herald of Truth, for it is TRUTH you proclaim! The adversary rages against you and all who labor in the vineyard, but in your complete trust you have found the key of your peace. It is the key that opens the hearts of

the Trinity to provide all your necessities and to guide you to those whose hearts are open to our call. It is imperative to proclaim this message and you will continue, while you are able, Tell me what you understand of the vision shown to you.

SJ: It is my understanding that the drawing of the Christian symbol by our Lord indicates the closeness of the time when we, too, will begin to identify ourselves one to another in a secret way, that persecution is soon upon humanity. The Holy Father is walking the Way of the Cross for the Church. John Paul II reads from the scroll the dogma which will be the catalyst that will place prophetic events in motion.

MARY: You are correct, my little sorrowful rose, and for this reason your mission intensifies. Do not fear. I will help you and God will sustain you by His power. You will see, in days ahead, events of a cataclysmic nature, so I implore you continue your prayer, your simple life of solitude, when you are not out evangelizing. That which you will see, will rock the soul of man and shake him so that he would fear his Maker! The Father is just and he will purify the world and his Church!

My Beloved Sons! You who are faithful, you are the jewels of my crown and I love you and protect your priestly vocation! You are not called to anything more than to be a witness! If you are holy, you will teach my children how to be holy. If you speak Truth, you will crush lies. If you are fearless, I will protect you, for though the enemy rages, he will not touch you! I will see to it, for I am the Woman who stands on the head of the serpent! If you would embody the Truth in one act, it is this: pray and offer the Holy Sacrifice of the Mass with your heart, so that the Father will be appeased and so that

Jesus will gaze back lovingly into your eyes, as lovingly as you gaze into His! It is time to do the fullness of battle with the enemy, soon to be revealed, you are going to be graced with blessings which require a re-dedication, do you accept?

SJ: I renounce all the world has to offer me and I give back to you all you have given me. Dispose of me according to your need and the Will of God, I will serve you and my God all the days of the rest of my life.

MARY: I will stand with you and protect you. I will be with you until the end. Do not fear. Never fear for what comes. There are angels who stand to do my bidding and the saints to assist you. I bless in a special way those who have assisted in any way to bring you here. The path of God's Will I will clearly illuminate, and in their heart they will know it is through my intercession that this has been obtained, I call you, my remnant, to continue and pray. Be assured of my protection and be at peace, We will continue later.

SJ: I was interrupted from taking the message here, Our Lady dismissed me and said we would continue later.

Message to Sadie Jaramillo – April 29, 1998, 3:50 p.m. (continued)

MARY: I am sent to do the Will of God whom I praise with you! My little sorrowful rose, we continue. You feel the opposition of the enemy; be at peace! I have you under my mantle of protection! Soon openly the princes

of the church will stand in opposition one to another and will fulfill prophecy given long ago. Openly they will begin to desecrate the sanctuaries of the church. You who have been called to recognize this will have the task of teaching those who are not aware of impending events. You must only fear God and not the judgment of man, if you have the love of My Son in the Eucharist, you will do as others who have been called to give witness to the Truth in the past have done. The rejection and denial of this Truth (Our Lord's being truly present in the Holy Eucharist), will be the reasons that darkness comes to the world! Look to the Vicar of Christ! Console yourselves with the teachings given to many. Live to the letter your consecrated life! I will prompt you at the proper time and you will alert the many and lead them through this time of darkness. Many are called to respond! DO SO, THAT MANY WILL BE SPARED! From within the Trinity, I obtain blessings for you and all who believe!

SJ: AMEN!

Many Will Receive Graces

<u>Message to Sadie Jaramillo – May 20, 1998, - June 14, 1998 – Feast of Corpus Christi</u>

My Beloved Sisters and Brothers in the Lord:

Many of you know that I returned from a pilgrimage that began on May 20th and ended June 5th. The following message has been given to me over the course of these days.

While I was on this pilgrimage, I prayed for all of you who pray for me. I prayed for all of you who have asked me to pray for you. This pilgrimage was not just for me, but rather, for you, and I will recount it for you very quickly. At Fatima, during the recitation of the Holy Rosary, I had the privilege of leading half of the fourth decade in English. While I prayed I couldn't believe I was actually there! Garabandal was my favorite place, second only to viewing the Holy Shroud at Turin. As I prayed at the pines on the top of the hill I could definitely feel Our Lady's presence. At Lourdes it turned out to be quite a surprise when my daughter Jazmine and I bathed in the healing waters. There was an inner healing waiting for the three of us, Chris, my son, had to go with the men, entrusted to Ted Ontiveras, a wonderful friend. I asked for physical healing for those who needed it from the many I was praying for. At Turin, in the midst of a furious downpour, and out of all the thousands of people there, we were in the very front row, as close to the Holy Shroud as anyone could possibly get! Then on to Assisi, Padua, Venice (and the tomb of St. Mark), Montichiari (the Shrine of Maria Rosa Mystica), and ending at Zaragoza (Our Lady of the Pillar)! I would have to write a book about all the experiences during this pilgrim-

age, but I wanted all of you to know that I took you with me in my heart, and in the book of petitions I laid at all these places.

I will mention that at Rome, May the 31st, Feast of Pentecost, there were thousands and thousands of pilgrims! I was only about a football field away from the Holy Father (which is better than being half-way around the world)! We have a man who one day will be declared a saint! While the proclamation of the Dogma was not made, he definitely said it in his homily! Perhaps this will be the first Dogma proclaimed in the Era of Peace!

With this introduction, I will begin to recount for you the message given to me by Our Lady. Peace! Do not fear!

Message given to Sadie Jaramillo – May 20, 1998, 10:50 a.m.

SJ: This part of the message was given to me on the plane.

MARY: I am your Victorious Queen of Heaven from whose womb was brought forth JESUS! WORD INCARNATE! PRAISE THE HOLY TRINITY! I call you to this mission of love, this mission of victory, this summit of my cohort! From every part of the continent will they gather to see, to hear the proclamation of this Dogma! But you will not see it! You who have labored diligently who have passed through the refiners fire, this is my gift of love, that I am crowned in your hearts!

From this title would fullness of power be granted, and my Triumph, in process now, would see great victories in

this battle of all battles! But you will not see it now for the enemies of God surround like evil vultures the Vicar of My Son! Remember you fight the prince of darkness, whom I will crush in victory under my heel in the end! The Vicar of My Son, weary under the weight of this cross, crosses over by means of the prayer rising from every corner of the world, the threshold! The Church, though eclipsed for the moment, will see the rising of hope and glory! You and others who have said yes to their Queen, will conquer with Me the powers of the anti-christ; He who lies ready to be revealed. Thus tremendous graces are poured forth on you and all who make this journey! Even now those who have played a role in the journey feel my presence and blessings!

Father J. stays (behind) to accomplish the Will of God the Father, to prepare what is needed! As he is open to the prompting of The Holy Spirit, he finds peace in every step, no matter how difficult. Be open to my leading for there are unexpected blessings for you. You will see the completion of your mission soon. For now, know I am ever near and you are in My Heart for My protection!

Message given to Sadie Jaramillo – May 23, 1998, 1:30 a.m.

MARY: The hour is late and we continue. I am your Mother who calls you to write; Jesus, My Son came in the flesh to redeem man! Praises to the Trinity!

Describe your vision.

SJ: During the rosary on the bus ride to Garabandal from Fatima, I was shown the sun, brilliantly shining, and there seemed to be a door which opens, like a curtain parting from the center. Our Lady comes forth, arrayed in a gown of light, with a magnificent crown, like Our Lady of Mercy's I thought.

She appears standing in the same position as the Virgin of Guadalupe, Her hands and gaze the same. Please bear with me. It is hard sometimes to describe what I am shown.

MARY: Now my little sorrowful rose, you go with my children on this pilgrimage of Love and as foretold to you, you have received unexpected graces, and you will receive more.

My children you are weary on this journey, but I will refresh you with the balm of My Motherly Love. Many will receive graces that will answer the desires of your hearts!

My daughter P. will receive the grace she asks for and her community will be fortified under my Love and protection. Continue to pray for her.

Carry in your hearts the prayers that grace has placed there. Be at peace, you will awaken refreshed under my motherly gaze. Peace child. We will continue later.

Message given to Sadie Jaramillo – May 24, 1998, 6:00 a.m.

SJ: During Sunday Mass at Garabandal I was shown again the same vision of Our Lady as described earlier in this message. She said, **"I will open doors that have up to now been closed."** I am awakened:

MARY: Tell my daughter A., "The cross has shown you that in the end, the Will of God prevails. I am the Daughter of His Will, who gave Jesus in the flesh to the world. Up to now the doors have been shut, (but) the cross symbolizes the Triumph of the Cross at Calvary. IT IS the Will of God, for these are the times of all times. You and M. and others who believe must prepare for the multitudes who will take refuge here. It is under my mantle of protection. Thus I have given you the sign seen by many last night to confirm this message. You know of My great love. Tell it! To all it must be told. Your peace will come from the acceptance of this that has already been shown to you. I bid you blessings from the Trinity."

SJ: AMEN.

Message given to me at Lourdes – May 25, 1998, 2:30 a.m.

SJ: During Holy Mass in the chapel of the Basilica I hear Our Lord speak. He says to me: **"My Daughter, console Me, for in these most holy of shrines, I have shown you, though you may see an ocean of people, few are they who live my law of love."**

MARY: From this most venerated shrine I prepared humanity to receive a river of graces for the healing of the spirit. My concern is that many come to seek the healing and not He who heals. These that you see are some of the multitudes who live the Way of the Cross. Their suffering united to our Two Hearts brings many graces to humanity, graces not asked for. You have seen my image as shown to you in the vision, triumphantly crowned. This triumph will be my title: Mary, Co-

Redemptrix, Mediatrix of all Graces. For I am a River of Light allowing the river of grace to flow to the hearts of my children, many of whom have closed their hearts to My Son and to Me. Those who cause our hearts the most grief are priests, sons of mine, brothers to My Son! If the confusion has reached in these holy places it is now that you see the truth spoken of long ago. **This journey, though difficult for many, covers My Son's vicar** (John Paul II) **with prayer, intercessory prayer, for he is walking the Way of the Cross with you. The images shown to you during the recitation of My Holy Rosary as you left Fatima indicate the nearness of the rise again of these enemies of the true faith.**

Note: I was shown two images, the hammer and sickle and a type of sword I did not recognize. During a period of sharing with some in my group, Ted described it perfectly. It is the sword used in the Masonic emblems. It definitely has something to do with the Islamic religion also. Along with this vision I also saw Our Lady as I described previously, but this time She was sitting and weeping. It was like the image I have seen of Our Lady of La Salette.

MARY: My little sorrowful rose, console the Hearts of the Mother and The Son. PRAY.

Message given to Sadie Jaramillo – May 26, 1998, 3:30 a.m.

SJ: Here I am reminded of what Our Lady said to me in Garabandal.

MARY: I kissed all that represented that which the enemy would seek to destroy. I kissed the crucifix's for My Son's Holy Sacrifice of the Mass which they would

seek to destroy. I kissed the habit against the destruction of orders and vocations. I blessed the bedrooms of families against the destruction of life in the womb and families, for from the marriage bed comes life! All these things the enemy has sought to destroy. Sleep child, we will continue later.

Message given to Sadie Jaramillo – June 8, 1998, 1:00 p.m.

MARY: My little sorrowful rose, it is I, your Mother, who enfolds you in Her Heart. Your suffering is necessary and united to the suffering Heart of Jesus, My Son, Word come in the flesh and to the Sorrows of My Immaculate Heart.

Note: Today I am in bed since early morning with a crown of thorns around my head, though they be invisible. One other time have I experienced this pain. My head feels hot and as though it will explode. Early afternoon, I begin to hear Our Lady, after testing the spirit, She reveals She wants me to write. As the pain is lifted, grace prevails to allow this message.

MARY: You will include the visions given to you on the pilgrimage. As the requests of My Heart have not been complied with, and as humanity continues to close both heart and ears to the Words of Heaven, I now announce to you that this will be the last public message given by me to you. This message will be given in its completed form by June 14th, 1998, (Feast of Corpus Christi). You will continue to be that sentinel keeping watch, and you will proclaim loudly and to all that which will be revealed (to you).

First, in regard to all those who made this pilgrimage: to the ones who assisted you and your children to be able to go; those who worked on this pilgrimage, your intentions have been received and placed on heaven's altar with the assurance that I, Co-Redemptrix and Mediatrix of all Graces, will obtain your heart's request in accordance with the Divine Will of God. Blessings were poured out in overflowing abundance on those who know the seriousness of this pilgrimage. Thus you were tested in endurance and perseverance. The many people and intentions carried in your heart and in the hearts of the others brings answers to those also.

Now I tell you <u>Mercy will come from the heavens and be revealed in the midst of great chaos and upheaval!</u>
The reality of words spoken prophetically long ago was shown to you at the many sites of apparition: the confusion, the division, the lack of love and reverence. But at the Sacrifice of the body and Blood of My Son, clear evidence is given.

I can reveal that **My Son's Vicar** (John Paul II) knows the truth behind the murder of his guard; most people do not. I can reveal that at the present time his (John Paul II) hands are tied in regard to the Dogma. But those who were there and heard know it is what is in his heart, and that he did say it. (In his homily on Pentecost Sunday). I can reveal that the enemies of God believe the victory is theirs! <u>But I tell you now this Triumph of Mine has been borne in the hearts of the most obscure and littlest of children. This Triumph will escalate and in the greatest battle of all battles, children of mine, I reveal again, I WILL STAND ON THE SERPENTS HEAD AND IMMOBILIZE ALL HIS EVIL FORCES, AND YOU MY LITTLE ONES WILL BE VICTORIOUS WITH ME!!</u>

Your suffering is necessary for the many who will continue to die in days ahead. Plead with me that these poor souls are given grace of conversion at the last moment.

Your Father in Heaven and Mine will no longer be mocked! He will no longer allow mankind to go unpunished. The deaths of many loom on the horizon! We will continue later child.

Message given to Sadie Jaramillo – June 14, 1998

MARY: My little sorrowful rose, the hour grows late and there is much to do. Yes, I dwell in the midst of the Trinity and with you praise GOD for the gift of MY son, flesh of MY flesh, yet Divinely God's Love!

I impress upon you these words: NOW WILL THE JUSTICE OF GOD CONTINUE TO FALL ON MANKIND!

This Feast of Corpus Christi, (celebrates) the essence of your life, (my Son's) Body, Blood, Soul and Divinity! This truth the enemies of God seek to destroy, yet I tell YOU the more this truth is denied the more I will call my remnant to defend it BY your witness of love! Many of MY requests down through the ages have not been complied with. This I have told YOU already. Nonetheless, my Triumph as Queen, Co-Redemptrix, Mediatrix was begun in the hearts of you, my remnant and priests of MY Heart, who are the jewels of My Crown!

I TELL YOU AGAIN THAT MERCY WILL DESCEND

AMIDST FIRE AND turmoil! The symbols shown to you on your trip indicate the red dragon will rear its ugly head and align itself with those of the race of the Orient! So too will the Freemasons make their move to accomplish their one-world order. Islam is a sleeping giant ready to awaken. Thus many in the coming days WILL PRAY FOR DEATH, FOR THESE HAVE NOT PREPARED FOR THIS BATTLE OF ALL BATTLES! The preparations are spiritual ones and many have spent precious time in only the cares of the world. They will find, as with many princes of the Church, that there IS a God, A GOD OF LOVE WHO ONLY ASKED FOR THEIR HEART! ALL that has been foretold to YOU and many others is on the point of being fulfilled. Know that I your Mother and the Mother of God, ask now from you the total focus of your heart on My son Jesus, for this apostasy which is eclipsing the Church will soon bring darkness and the fulfillment of Daniel's prophecy. (Daniel Chapter 12) The one who has prepared snares and traps for humanity prepares for his unveiling to the world. Peace, security and wealth he will promise, and order to a world filled with disorder! The message YOU proclaim is to awaken the dead souls of MY children to the truth.

My children, beware of the lures of satan, for he fills you with prophets of deceit to divide and lure you from the Truth! HUMANITY, YOU WILL WEEP TEARS AND TEARS OF BLOOD!! WOE TO YOU WHO STILL WANDER ABOUT WITH NO LIFE IN YOU! But mercy, if you accept, will bring life to your souls, life filed with repentance and remorse.

CHOOSE LIFE MY CHILDREN, ON THIS FEAST WHICH COMMEMORATES EVERLASTING LIFE! NOW YOU, MY CHILDREN, WHO HAVE NOT

BELIEVED WILL BELIEVE, BECAUSE YOU WILL SEE WITH YOUR HEART THE REALITY OF MY WARNINGS OF LOVE!

I bid you peace my little sorrowful rose. Blessings to you and all who believe!!!

SJ: Amen.

My Children Prepare For What Comes

<u>Message Given to Sadie Jaramillo – July 7, 1998, 10:30 p.m.</u>

Beginning letter:

My Dear Brothers and Sisters in Christ:

Many have expressed dismay that I have been told by Our Lord and Our Lady that the public messages to me have ended. I would like to explain what that means to both me and you.

If you go back and read the early messages you will find that Our Lord and Lady were still imploring their children to convert, reconcile themselves to their God and begin to walk the Way of the Cross. Many would believe that all the prophecies of "doom and gloom" are empty and will never happen. Well I tell you now, my brothers and sisters, look around at the events now happening in the world. We have been living in a time of mercy.

Now the messages are basically revealing what the Lord is showing me will happen. I have not stopped receiving "communications" from the Lord and/or Our Lady. They have charged me with the responsibility of being the "sentinel in the watchtower to alert God's children."

Therefore, the messages they are giving are not frequent, but they are encouraging us to PERSEVERE! I have been given the responsibility of warning all of you, who believe, of what the Lord is showing me. I will continue to do so until that time (which WILL arrive) that I can no longer do so.

Update news on this House of Prayer: we will be filing the Articles of Incorporation as a non-profit religious corporation within this next week. We'll then file state and federal application for tax-exempt status. For all of you who have given to this Apostolate, I carry you in my heart every day to Our Lord and Our Lady. By their promises, not mine, they have said it will obtain special graces in these difficult days for all who participate. I need you. I need your prayers. But more than that, I IMPLORE YOU, CONTINUE TO PRAY FOR PRIESTS!!!!!

My brothers and sisters, be at peace! Let no one rob you of your peace! Keep the Joy of the Lord in your hearts! What we have to go through is to take us to the time when we will live enveloped in the Eucharistic Love of Jesus, and the Triumph of the Immaculate Heart of Mary! Whatever we go through will be infinitely better then what we have now.

I AM UNITED WITH YOU IN PRAYER AND IN THE LOVE OF JESUS AND MARY,

Sadie j.

Message Given to Sadie Jaramillo – July 7, 1998:

JESUS: My Mother's little sorrowful rose, describe your visions, for I who am Love Incarnate and the Word Incarnate ask you to do this. I WHO AM Flesh of My Mother's flesh, Praise My Father!

SJ: I have been shown for the last two and a half weeks a crescent moon with a star. Then I see the moon crack in half, the bottom half falling away from the top half, but still connected. I then see a river of blood begin to flow from the bottom half of the moon.

One week ago today, while praying in the cenacle, I see a flash of fire, or something that looks very hot. It is more straight than round and has fumes rising from it, like gas fumes rising. It is like a flare that they shoot to show a location. I don't know from where it has come for I can only see where it is headed, and that is to earth. I see earth off in the distance. Please bear with me when describing these visions. It is very hard sometimes.

JESUS: Now I, WHO AM the lover of your soul, will reveal the meaning of these visions. The symbol of Islam indicates the river of blood that will flow from the instigation of war by these nations. They will also cause here in this country racial and civil strife and unrest. The second vision indicates the signs from the heavens as spoken of in scripture that will cause these bursts of fire to fall upon a humanity out of sync with its God! (Mt 24:29) **Humanity has reached the level of degradation that has surpassed that of any other time! By their "knowledge" they believe they have no need for their Creator!**

Well, by My Power I will uncover the shame of my shepherds who lead my people astray, who teach too many lies given birth to in the very pit of hell! My people will lament and wail, cry tears, and bear sorrows! I ask you to alert my children. TELL THEM THAT IF THEY PRAY, IF THEY ARE RECONCILED TO ME, IF THEY ARE BOUND TO THE TWO HEARTS, BY THE SPIRIT OF GOD THEY WILL BE LED, AND PROTECTED.

My children you are weary, but My Word says IF YOU PERSEVERE, ONLY THEN WILL YOU BE SAVED!

What I say to you now is this: You would not come to ME, for your heart is hard, so now my justice will fall and bend your stiff necks!!

My shepherds! I Who see all, know all. I KNOW OF YOUR DEEDS THAT ARE SHAMEFUL! Thus I send this small voice crying out in the desert of the dryness of my children's hearts to proclaim what you no longer proclaim! YOUR SINS have brought this to humanity!

Now child, recall the vision shown to you before:

SJ: I recall a time when I was shown an image of the world, a globe. Then I saw this globe move ever so slightly from its normal position.

JESUS: These atomic bombs which have been set off, cause the very bowels of the earth to shift. Thus the world WILL suffer for the foolishness of man. The weather ceases to have seasons and unusual weather phenomena will become more and more prevalent! These are just the beginnings! The earth will shift and give vent to the just anger of God! Many of my children will come to you seeking counsel and consolation. Teach them my children, for the preparations have been made. What is not finished, I WILL DO!

MY CHILDREN PREPARE FOR WHAT COMES! Listen to this small voice, one of many that has been lifted up to give my warnings of Love!

Do not fear. We are with you and all who believe!

Continue to pray for My brother priests, that they return their hearts to their God!

With my Father who loves and has given the world Love Incarnate, with the Spirit, Holy and Powerful, WE Bless you and all who believe!

SJ: AMEN.

A Great Outpouring Of My Spirit

<u>Message Given to Sadie Jaramillo – August 15, 1998, 12:30 a.m. – Feast of the Assumption of the Blessed Virgin Mary</u>

JESUS: I Jesus, lover of your soul, proclaim to all: I came once in the flesh and walked in the midst of man. I announce to you: SOON, YOU WILL SEE ME COME ON THE CLOUDS IN GLORY TO RE-ESTABLISH A TIME OF PEACE FOR MANKIND!

Praise, Honor and Glory to the Blessed Trinity!!

My Mother's little sorrowful rose, write your visions:

SJ: Within the last month and a half I have been shown several visions. They are as follows:

Approximately 5 weeks ago I am shown what appears to be boiling lava, and I can see it rising upward. I hear the words "magma," "Helen" and "Mammoth." I then see a book. The title of the book is "Word of God." Then the book opens and by a force not seen by me, it is torn in half. The Lord then brings to my mind the opening verses of the Gospel of St. John: "In the beginning was the word: the Word was in God's presence, and the Word was God. He was present to God in the beginning. Through Him all things came into being, and apart from him nothing came to be." John 1:1

I am given the understanding that this refers to the Word of God being Jesus, and Jesus' body (the church) being split in two. This is an indication of the schism that will occur soon. That is why the Holy Father recently clarified what we, the faithful, are obliged to believe. He is clearly defining important doctrines so that God's people will not be confused.

The word magma is the lava under the earth, before an eruption. The words Helen and Mammoth refer to the two volcanoes which will be a sign for the believers.

Four weeks ago I am awakened hearing the words: "The winds will be in excess of 100 mph. There is a storm coming that will be unexpected." Then the Lord reminds me that sometime during winter He had told me that three storms would come. Two storms came. I had forgotten about this word that had been given to me. He reminded me, and I had not thought that a storm could come at any other time other than winter. However, with these summer storms He gives me the understanding that the third one will come. He had told me that when I saw the three storms then I should know that we are in the time of seeing the trials of the tribulation increased and accelerated.

Three weeks ago I was shown a vision of myself, dressed in a white gown, with long hair and definitely younger than I am now. I saw myself running with my arms open to Jesus, into His arms, open to receive me. I then looked over to the side of this vision and I saw myself as I am now. My body was lying lifeless on the ground. I do not know how death will come. But knowing that this is a very real possibility does not scare me. Our goal is to be with the Lord for all eternity. When and how we get there is not all that is important. No matter how wonderful it will be in the Era of Peace, to be with the Lord surpasses all things.

Two weeks ago I was shown an image of a priest. Three very large angels were assisting this priest. They were helping him put on some armor. I especially saw them assisting him with a breastplate, and fastening some sandals.

Our Lord continues:

JESUS: You have written of your visions, revealed to you that you might call many to the action of prayer. The prayer you let rise from your heart will bear much fruit for the critical days ahead.

On this day that commemorates The Assumption of My Mother into heaven, Her beloved cohort gathers all around the world to let their voices rise in prayer and song, so that the prayers of the just might availeth much.

There is a foreboding silence that is deafening to the spiritually awake. You must recall my scripture; "The Day of the Lord will come as a thief... ." (2 Peter 3:10), and again, "Just when they are saying peace and security, ruin will befall them... ." (1 Thes.5:3) You have been shown the enemy that will cause the river of blood to rise. Their reign of terror plays right into the plan of those who will control (the world).

Mass confusion, great chaos, as my Father's hand of Justice falls! For these days you (and others) have been led; you have been prepared.

My Brother F. and many more like him will lead the flock, frightened, when they have struck the shepherd. My Vicar prepared to set the plan in motion, which will bring him much opposition and cause his enemies to seek to destroy him. Quickly he will have to flee! This he does by clearly defining the TRUTH! As he defines the TRUTH, those enemies who deny it (TRUTH) will seek to destroy him.

I am preparing to send forth a Great outpouring of My Spirit! I will renew hearts and anoint my priests, my brothers! Greater than ever before will be my assistance, so great is My Love for you!! Kings and kingdoms will fall, as prey for the vultures!!

SJ: I see the Richter scale indicating a great earthquake by the intense movement of the needle. I have been shown this before.

JESUS: The storms, volcanoes, earthquakes and wars are the means by which mankind will be brought to its knees!!

But you, My Mother's remnant, are kept in the "eye of the storm." Look neither to the left nor the right. Fasten your gaze to mine and you and many more will be given great courage so that even those gone before you (saints in heaven) **will rejoice at the level of heroic action many will rise to!!**

If my Light which will shatter the consciences of man is not accepted, then what more can I do that I haven't done already? This silence will be shattered by many events, so that it will seem many are happening at the same time!!

This Cross (the "Cross of Peace" project, Santa Maria, CA)**, one of many projects, has been sorely tested and the tempter who is My enemy seeks to destroy** (it)**. But because of the prayers, many of my children will marvel at what prevails quickly!**

Surrender your all to Me and to My Mother that you will continue to be our instrument.

Your family quickly comes!

My little apostles of Love live in MY LOVE, AND IN MY PEACE!

FROM HEAVEN'S THRONE, WE BLESS YOU AND ALL WHO BELIEVE!

SJ: AMEN!

SJ: NOTE TO THIS MESSAGE:

For the believer, please understand that even though we are told about coming chastisements, ALL IS CONDITIONAL ON YOUR RESPONSE!! The Lord told me that I have been shown the volcanoes erupting, and the great chasms caused by the earthquake, the storms, etc., so that I will remain prostrate on my face in prayer, beseeching the Father for Mercy!! We can still, and MUST pray!!! All has been foretold so that we will NOT be caught unaware! However we have a responsibility. IF WE BELIEVE AND ARE LIVING THE MESSAGES WE MUST TAKE ACTION!! YOU MUST PRAY FOR THE PRIESTS AND FOR OUR HOLY FATHER JOHN PAUL II!

The sin of abortion is calling down the Father's just hand! Please, please, do what you can. October the 13th will be an International Day of Prayer asking Our Lady of Guadalupe to bring an end to this scourge of abortion. It will be preceded by nine days of celebrating the Holy Eucharist, praying the Holy Rosary, and fasting. Organize, get together and join this crucial Novena and Day of Prayer that the Blessed Mother will be used as God's powerful instrument to end abortion.

Do not think that these punishments are not going to come! But we can still make a difference. We are a holy remnant of prayer warriors, not frightened children! There is no demon in hell that can prevail over the Lord and the Queen of Heaven who has already assured us of VICTORY!! MY BROTHERS AND SISTERS IN THE LORD, UNITE WITH ME AND MANY MORE, FOR THE DAYS AHEAD REQUIRE THIS OF US.

I am united with you in prayer,

Love in the Most Blessed Trinity,

Sadie Jaramillo

My People Perish For Lack of Knowledge

<u>Messages to Sadie Jaramillo – August 21-25 1998</u>

SJ: I am given the following vision during mass on Friday, August 21, 1998:

I can see the hammer; sickle and Masonic sword (also the emblem for the Islamic religion) spread out like a fan. Then in one movement like a fan closing, they are all in line, one behind another, so it appears as if they are one image. Then, below this I can see an image of a globe. Suddenly it looks as if there is blood running down the globe.

The following visions were shown to me during a MMP cenacle on Saturday, August 22, 1998, Feast of the Queenship of Mary. They were shown to me in very rapid succession:

In the first vision I am shown a huge flash of lightning, about three strikes, very WIDE bolts, larger than anything I have ever seen as lightning strikes.

I then am shown a very HIGH tidal wave, and much water.

Next I am shown an arena, and the bottom is filled with people running in complete, chaotic frenzy. They are running into each other and seem to be filled with fear, for the looks on their faces indicate intense fear. I then am shown the top of this arena. At the top there are positioned evenly around people who are all gazing in the same direction, upwards. They seem to be strong, and in a position of one going into battle, as people who are vigilantly watching for a sign.

I then recognize the same vision of the hammer, sickle and the sword that resembles the Masonic sword, shown to me yesterday. They are spread out like a fan. Then they all seem to become one, as in the movement of closing a fan. Again I see the globe that seems to have blood running down it. Quite suddenly there is an illuminated cross in the heavens above the globe, above the symbols!

In the last vision I see flags of many nations. They are fanned out so that they are all visible. Then they begin to fall in line, behind the first one. Then a larger flag, totally black covers the other flags completely, so they are no longer seen. Only the black flag is seen which suddenly has a design of white stocks of wheat, which I recognize as the symbol for the United Nations.

On Monday, August 24, 1998, after receiving Holy Communion, I am given the following:

I am shown first a white cloud, large in size. Then as a wind begins to blow away the cloud I see God the Father in the cloud from the waist up. He looks just like Jesus, only with white hair. He is holding a rod in his hand that is raised. He is looking downward and the look on his face is very intense: not anger, but very JUST AND STERN. To the right side of this vision I see Jesus standing by Our Lady. Our Lady is lifting her mantle, as if to give refuge to a child.

The following message has been given to me in two parts. They are as follows:

Message given to Sadie Jaramillo – August 23, 1998, 10:30 p.m.

MARY: My little sorrowful rose, I your Queen and Mother of Christ Crucified, Christ Resurrected, pro-

claim: "As My Son came once in the flesh and lived among men, He prepares to Come Again in Glory to the Praise, Glory and Honor of the Blessed Trinity!!"

I receive your prayers and sufferings with great joy, for in this final hour much is granted because of this. (Offering of prayers and suffering on this particular day with a severe headache).

You are overwhelmed by visions shown to you before, revealed to you again! How rapidly in succession these visions are shown to you indicates how quickly will this and more come upon humanity!

Holy scripture says, "my people perish for lack of knowledge... ." (Hosea 4:6) This indicates what is becoming of my remnant, because they fill themselves with what will NOT withstand the wiles of the enemy! Thus the vision of the people running in all directions and in great fear indicates the great confusion that has come upon my remnant, because of the many false prophets. The few who seem prepared and strong (in the vision) are those whose gazes are on the TWO HEARTS! False prophets cause much harm to the body (of believers), but these will be unmasked and uncovered! If they DO NOT repent (they) will be cast aside and because of pride suffer eternal punishment!

Yes, retaliation will come to man for his folly! The errors of Russia, spoken of by Me at Fatima, have continued to be spread and lie hidden behind many masks, though it is the same enemy! But evil will unite with evil and the forces of the one world quickly unite behind the flag of evil (and) the man of iniquity is revealed (soon)!

SJ: At this point I could not continue to write, for I

became physically ill, due to the severe headache. Our Lady dismissed me and said She would continue later.

Message given to Sadie Jaramillo – August 25, 1998, 10:30 p.m.

MARY: My little sorrowful rose let us continue that My words of urgency will be sent to my children. Recall you have been called to be the sentinel in the watchtower!

Yes, it is I, your heavenly Mother and Queen, who dwells in the midst of the Most Holy and Blessed Trinity! I along with all the saints sing praises to the Holy One True God!! My Son lived amongst men, and prepares to come again. HE WILL ESTABLISH THE TIME OF PEACE FOR MANKIND!! These visions are for you to understand the fulfillment of words given to you and many others, in terms that you understand, that soon the illumination of your conscience and the state of your soul will occur! Has it not been told to you that this great event would come in the midst of great chaos and confusion? Then continue my little children to come to me in prayer! Continue to come to me with all of your sufferings, taking refuge in My Immaculate Heart and under My Mantle! Quickly will the Father's Justice be upon humanity, and that will make all that has happened up to now pale in comparison. NOW is the time for you to make a difference!

Those in the vision who seem strong are my prayer warriors, who know and believe with all their being that I will obtain all from the Most Blessed Trinity for you, my children. They have their gazes fastened on Me and My Son, JESUS! TRUST MY CHILDREN! TRUST that our promises are tried and true!

I implore you for your prayers for my beloved priest sons, jewels of my crown! Oh if they knew my great love for them! If they knew how I long to assist them! To do the Will of the Father is to BECOME HOLY, AND TO TEACH MY CHILDREN TO BE HOLY, to be little and not puffed up with pride!

Your prayers and sufferings, my remnant, enable much to be done for the body of Christ! Continue to pray, focused on prayer, and NOT punishments! The punishments are not for Gods children, BUT FOR HIS ENEMIES!

I came to show you the WAY BACK AGAIN, TO MY SON! YOU MUST TRUST, AND IF YOU HAVE FORGOTTEN, YOU MUST REMEMBER TO TRUST, TRUST, TRUST IN WHAT JESUS WILL DO FOR YOU! You are ASSURED of my promises to keep and protect you, if you will give me your permission, your fiat, just as I gave mine to the Father!

Many of you, my children, are awaiting the arrival of a sign that will signal to you the beginning of calamities. But you must know that you HAVE BEEN IN AND ARE ARRIVING TO THE HEIGHT of the MOST DIFFICULT PERIOD, the TIME OF ALL TIMES! No other time compares to these times!

Thus you see (in the vision) the Hand of the Father's Justice raised upon mankind! You also see Me still allowing my children to take refuge in My Immaculate Heart and Under My Mantle! My Son, Jesus, who did all that He could for humanity on Calvary, stands by My side.

Take refuge my children, take refuge. In My Heart I will lead you, I will guide you. But you must pray! Pray much for guidance, and discernment.

I obtain blessings from the Trinity for you and for all who BELIEVE!

SJ: AMEN.

The Father's House of Victory Through the Holy Family

On September 20, 1997, Our Lady gave Sadie a message to establish "The Father's House of Victory Through the Holy Family" Apostolate. Following is that message:

Mary: I did not bring you here (Santa Maria) **to start another prayer group. I brought you here to form the beginning of many prayer communities to receive and to teach the many who will come to take refuge under this "Cross of Peace." I am addressing you as Our Lady of Victory through the Holy Rosary to give Glory and Praise to God the Eternal Father and Victory for the Holy Family!**

You shall call this apostolate: "The Father's House of Victory Through the Holy Family!"

You will embrace the Seven Virtues of the Holy Spirit and be the instrument to teach and do the Seven Corporal Works of Mercy, (and) **you will console the Seven Sorrows of Mary! This shall be done by the Perpetual Adoration of Jesus in the Eucharist! True God and True Man! And by all the ways I have come to announce to all to pick up your weapon, the Holy Rosary, and wear your armor, the Scapular!**

You will by lot (choosing lots)**, but first prayer and fasting, choose from those faithful to your group of prayer to be the governing body of this Apostolate. Your director will continue with the help of God to lead and guide through correct counsel. The house will come first and soon the people to come later** (physically).

Let me explain the title: The Father's House Is a house of prayer, for scripture says, "My house shall be a house of prayer." (Matthew 21:13) **As the darkness pervades ever more in the sanctuaries of His Church, these small but powerful groups will continually keep the Light of Faith, the Light of Truth, the Light of**

Hope in the days of distress to come. Victory, for the victory comes from prayer, fasting and boldly proclaiming Truth in the face of lies. Victory comes with unity, and with unity comes unselfish acts of heroics that gives Glory to God!

I have proclaimed in all My valid apparitions victory would come through the small, the humble, the childlike who respond to the Mother's request of prayer, fasting, conversion, repentance and reparation, who unceasingly pray the powerful rosary!

The Holy Family is the Father's Great Gift to mankind! I, who dwell in the midst, am called: Daughter of the Father, Mother of the Son, Spouse of the Holy Spirit. It is the Trinity that is blessed, worshipped and praised, each for their great manifestations of love on mankind.

How the Father's Love is great to allow Jesus so great to become so little, so that the sin of death to the soul could be erased in the living waters of baptism and the blood of the perfect and unspotted lamb, (and) Jesus in the arms of his earthly father, My chaste spouse and saint, Joseph.

Knowing the sanctity of family life, as intended by God, would be sorely attacked and families would lie wounded, scattered and bruised – the visible representation on earth of the Heavenly Jesus, Mary and Joseph!

But the victory of God will bring together that great Truth once again and the Family of Nazareth will be the pattern for all in the coming era! I, as the woman who stands on the head of the serpent, will bring about this victory in the hidden hearts and lives of My faithful.

We enter into the fullness of this battle.

In this house you will receive the broken, console and comfort the frightened and help prepare them (teach). The people who will come will come to assist in the works that consist of the corporal works of mercy. First and foremost, you will minister to My Sons Beloved Brother Priests. This can only come about if you believe with the faith of a child. I am arranging all through the hearts open to Me.

The Father's House of Victory Through the Holy Family

SADIE & FATHER JIM

Sadie Jaramillo and Fr. Jim Anderson, M.S.A., her spiritual director, at the entrance to "The Father's House of Victory Through the Holy Family" in Santa Maria, California. Father Jim is a member of The Missionaries of the Holy Apostles and a retired Navy chaplain. He has been a priest twenty years with assignments teaching high school and seminary courses in ethics, including posts as Academic Dean and Academic Vice President of Holy Apostles Seminary in Cromwell, CT. He is a former attorney with a J.D. in law from U.C. Berkeley and a Ph.D. in philosophy from Georgetown University.

THE HOLY EUCHARIST

Private celebration of Holy Eucharist followed by recitation of the Rosary for the Church and for the intentions of associates, friends and guests of the Father's House of Victory Through the Holy Family.

SPIRITUAL GROWTH

Members, associates and guests of the Father's House of Victory Through the Holy Family gathered for weekly prayer and study of the sacred scriptures.

Youth of the Father's House of Victory Through the Holy Family make study and prayer fun, as they grow spiritually, socially and emotionally.

PRAYERS & QUESTIONS

Sadie devotes long hours praying with callers and guests, and answering their many questions concerning the messages and visions she has received. She can be contacted by phone at (805) 928-3994

between the hours of 10:00 a.m. and 9:00 p.m., United States, Pacific Coast Time. She maintains her own speaking and travel schedule. The World Wide Web site address of The Father's House of Victory Through the Holy Family is www.fathersvictory.org. Sadie's e-mail address is sorrowfulr@fathersvictory.org.

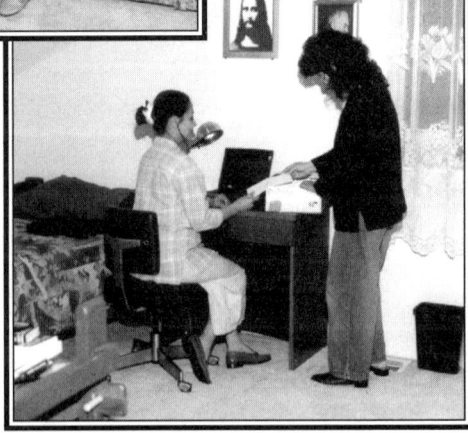

CROSS OF PEACE PILGRIMS

Sadie speaking to and praying with pilgrims to the Cross of Peace gathering to Storm Heaven with Prayer for the Jubilee Year 2,000, for the land Mary has designated for the Cross of Peace, and for the solemn papal proclamation that Mary is Co-redeemer, at Preisker Park in Santa Maria September 12, 1999.

Sadie with two of her children Jazmine and Chris and their dog Max

Picture of planned Cross of Peace Project at Santa Maria, California

I Will Lead! I Will Gather! I Will Protect!

<u>Message to Sadie Jaramillo – September 24, 1998 – Our Lady of Ransom</u>

SJ: I was awakened yesterday morning, hearing what Our Lady had been speaking gently all through the night. I had been reluctant to take this message for the fear I always have that the message might not be coming from the Lord.

I had in my morning prayers gone to the Lord and asked for a sign. In the depths of my heart I said, "Lord you do not leave me alone, but I asked you for a sign." Still I could hear Him asking me to take Our Lady's words. I sat at my desk which has a picture of Jesus and Padre Pio over it. Again in my heart I said, "Lord, I will not write until you speak, in Your Word, to me to give me the assurance I seek. I am weak I know." I grabbed my Bible and began to cry, and pray. I placed myself before The Trinity. I could see Jesus, The Father, and a mist of Light (The Holy Spirit). Immediately I heard, "First Thessalonians, chapter two." I opened to the scripture given by the Lord and read what spoke to my heart:

1 Thess. 2:3-4: "The exhortation we deliver does not spring from deceit or impure motives or any sort of trickery; rather, having met the test imposed on us by God, as men entrusted with the good tidings, we speak like those who strive to please God, 'the tester of our hearts,' rather than men."

SJ: How foolish I am! But how wonderful God is! Our Lady began:

MARY: My little sorrowful rose, I am the Mother of

Sorrows, who brought forth from my womb the man called JESUS, who would be called "The Man of Sorrows." Behold the Man! (Ecce Homo!) I praise the Most Holy and Sacred Trinity for the gift to be the Mother, and for the gift of "The Son!"

Behold my little sorrowful rose, through my motherly tears of sorrow I behold (know) what will befall (come to) humanity!

Describe your visions:

SJ: This vision pertains to the Cross of Peace, which I saw lying on its side, resting on the crossbeam. On one side I saw a group of people. On the other side a group of angels. There is a rope that both sides are pulling on. I can't see where the rope comes from. Then slowly the cross begins to rise.

In my second vision I am at mass making my thanksgiving after receiving Holy Communion. I see a man dressed as one of the hierarchy of the church, like a cardinal or bishop. I am then shown his heart, which is very black and entwined around his heart is a serpent. I am taken aback, and as I lift my head my gaze falls on the open tabernacle. It is still empty, for the priest has not placed the ciborium back inside. I hear the Lord say to me, **"Weep with Me, my child, for soon they will change the words they pronounce and they will not call my presence down!"**

In my 3rd vision I am shown the leader of a Muslim nation, whom I **do** recognize. He is standing next to a man who is dressed all in white, with a turban and long coat or something like that. He is very tall compared to the other man. His back is to me. The one I recognize has a smile and he appears to be introducing him to some others who are present. I am given the understanding that this man in white is the anti-christ, and soon will come on the scene. He is dressed in white because he will come as a "wolf in sheep's clothing." I cannot see, but am given the understanding that there seems to be chaos around the world because of some very grave event that has happened.

Our Lady continues:

MARY: I wish to tell my children the battle of all battles, the time of all times is come. Many times and through many vessels my motherly requests and implorations have for the most part gone UNHEEDED. **What more can I do for you my children, that I have not done already?**

You live in this moment of time when the leaders of many nations cry, "There is peace. There is security." They (the leaders) **of this elite hierarchy that places itself directly against the Church, holy and true, and against the world, continue to plot and pull the strings that are giving a "false" sense of security and peace. My children have been lulled to sleep and we have the blind leading the blind. The conscience of humanity is so dulled by the barrage of lies that the "silent slaughter"** (abortion) **goes on.**

There are a few voices "crying in the wilderness" and woe to those who have heard and not recognized this time of their visitation. You see the beginning, the birth pangs, of the merciful cleansing from Gods Justice! Do not think that it comes from any other source! Thus the Vicar of Christ in his recent and powerful clarifications on matters of the Faith, CLEARLY SUBSTANTIATED AND SET FORTH WHAT THE FAITHFUL, MY REMNANT, ARE CALLED TO DO! Do not look to any

other as your leader and your guide. JOHN PAUL II GUIDES WITH ALL THE FORCE OF CHRIST, WHOM HE REPRESENTS!

IN THE MIDST OF ALL THESE STORMS THAT MIRROR THE FURY OF GODS WRATH, WILL COME YOUR MERCIFUL ACT OF WARNING FOR HUMANITY! Before the year is over you will see the fulfillment of past prophecy. My children will be stripped of worldly possessions and means, that they might discover the "pearl of great price" (Jesus).

To you my children who are faithful, mingle your tears with mine and I will gather them all as precious jewels and deliver them to the Father, for my promises, as the promises of My Son, are faithful and True! I will lead! I will gather! I will protect! I will be at the sides of many who will be called to give witness!

The more the enemies seek to silence my children the more bold you will become. The prayers that rise are the fragrant offering consoling the Sorrows of Mary, consoling the Sorrows of My Son Jesus!

As you continue to pray for my project, already the answers and those who will come by the promptings placed in their hearts and spirits, are being brought together, (so) that this Cross of Peace will become a beacon of light and hope that will break through the darkness that comes. It will rise with the assistance of the angels because Divine Providence will remove obstacles and intervene in this project that will rise over this valley that bears my name (Santa Maria).

Through my eyes as the Mother of Sorrows, I clearly see what comes shortly to humanity! The anti-christ and his forces will come on this scene of confusion in the world and more confusion in the Church. IF IT WERE NOT FOR "DIVINE MERCY" many more of my children and priest sons would fall into the abyss of deception and misery, and ultimate damnation!

You are held in the silence to atone, to be purified, and to continue even the nothingness of your life, as a continual act of co-partnership with Me, your Mother, and together all the little nothings, in the name of Love (Jesus), **bring the assured victory!**

All who participate bring unto themselves and their loved ones, great graces showered for the dark days of trial ahead.

Lift up your hearts my children, strengthen your droopy knees in the Truth, **JESUS YOUR KING, LORD AND SAVIOR COMES SOON!!**

I bless you, with all who believe In the Name of My Father, and yours, My Son, Jesus, and The Most Holy Spirit!

SJ: AMEN, AMEN, AMEN.

NOTE TO THIS MESSAGE:

There yet remains to go through the extreme fullness of the "bloody trial." If you have not reconciled yourself to God through his sacraments, if you have not made your peace with your enemies, if your strength is not through the Eucharist, then I implore you, the nobody that I am, to please do so soon. Nothing since the beginning of humanity has come upon the world like what lies ahead for us. None of this makes any sense if you do not KNOW Jesus and Our Lady. I mean really, personally, in your heart.

How many messages talk about prayer of the heart? That merely means, my brothers and sisters, opening the gift we received at baptism. At some point in your life you need to invite the reality of Jesus and Our Lady into your life. It is a prayer of surrender, and humility, for you are acknowledging that even your intellect is nothing without Jesus and the Seat of Wisdom, Our Lady!

I am united with you, the many who are on the "battlefront," and those hidden "in the nothingness of your lives." Together with Our Lady and Our Lord, WE WILL TRIUMPH.

PRAY, PRAY, PRAY!

United with you in prayer,

Sadie Jaramillo

Woe To The Hardened Of Heart!

<u>Message given to Sadie Jaramillo – October 25, 1998, – 9:00 a.m.</u>

SJ: I begin to hear Our Lord, and I test, which I always do, according to the scriptures. Our Lord instructs me to please write the vision that I have been seeing for about three weeks.

Our Lord answers me as follows:

JESUS: I AM THE ALPHA AND THE OMEGA, THE FIRST AND THE LAST, THE ONE WHO WILL COME AGAIN SOON, AS I CAME ONCE IN THE FLESH, TO BRING SALVATION TO MANKIND! WITH YOU, I PRAISE THE FATHER FOR HIS GREAT LOVE!!

My Mother's little sorrowful rose, write your vision:

SJ: For the past three weeks, I have seen at various times the following vision:

It is of the world. Then, from the top, a light begins to shine and break through the heavens very slowly. Then, little by little, the light is shining upon the whole globe. I then see the illuminated cross which has been shown to me before in the heavens. I then understand that the light has come from the cross.

This morning I am shown a vision of the ocean. I am in a house that has a window facing the ocean. I am shown first of all the sea, as a normal scene. Then I see the waves begin to get more frightful, and I am shown a wave that will break over the house I am in. Nobody believes me when I begin to tell them what is going to happen. Then this wave hits, and everyone is trying to get out at the same time. I look at a floor in the house and I can see it like the water of the ocean. The vision ends.

JESUS: Now my child, I tell you hell hath no fury that will compare to the fury (that will be) **unleashed by the Omnipotent Father by permitting those who have remained obstinate to be placed under the yoke of control! Control that many foolishly believe cannot be** (real)**.**

But I HAVE heard the cries of sorrow and the call of the righteous, who are justified by the acknowledgment of their sinfulness. Your cries I have heard! For I know the evil that abounds and is rising still. You who cry out to call on Gods Justice, your cries I have heard!

Just as you are shown this light that will illuminate the heart and soul of every man, woman, and child, every pagan, every Jew, NONE will be left without recourse to My Mercy!!

BUT WOE AND AGAIN WOE to the hardened of heart! Woe to those who minister in my name! WOE to you who do not receive this act of Mercy and Love, and bring not only yourselves, but your flocks safely into the harbor of TRUTH! WOE to you who speak in my name, but I DO NOT SPEAK TO YOU!

The shower of stars brings many cosmic events which will bring the Warning to your soul!

If you cannot understand with your head then remem-

ber God's ways speak to the HEARTS of man!

You are being inspired by my Most Holy Spirit to rise to this occasion. You and many more will give witness!

Take for now each moment as precious **GRACE AND MERCY** obtained (by My Mother) **so truly the length of time under the yoke of control will be shortened!**

I have revealed to you it is the Masonic forces united with Islam and communism that will wreak havoc on the world! Terrorism, strategically planned, will bring this nation to its knees! Your leader, with others, play at acquiring peace, yet peace will not come!

Be warriors, ready for the battle. Be vigilant, for by your prayers that do rise as the sound of thundering water, graces and SPECIAL graces for the days ahead are given in the cenacle!

Not much longer and humanity will know the judgement!

Not much longer and the whirlwind of storms and natural disasters will break!

Not much longer and money and materials will be of no avail (use)!

Pray, my Mother's remnant. Give thanks for the shortening of this time! I bless you and all who believe. I encourage you to find PEACE IN MY HEART! DO NOT FEAR, YOU ARE MINE!

SJ:	AMEN, AMEN, AMEN.

Note To This Message:

Clearly, Our Lord refers to the warning that is upon all of humanity. But, more importantly, that the cenacle is where we are given the graces to understand the signs that the whole world is blind to. Of course, this is AFTER daily mass, being in a state of grace, and frequent confession. KEEP PRAYING, UNITED IF YOU CAN, WITH OTHERS! PRAY THE CONSECRATION GIVEN TO FATHER GOBBI, THROUGH THE MMP!! (Marian Movement of Priests)

Our Lady gives FOUR VERY IMPORTANT PROMISES THROUGH THIS MOVEMENT!

They are as follows:

1. She will strengthen the bonds of matrimony. People in satanic cults FAST for the breakup of families! If you are married you will not make it in these days without Our Lady's protection!

2. She will save all your children. Even if it looks hopeless to you, for Our Lady, it is easy! The Blessed Trinity CANNOT SAY NO TO HER!! Bind your children to the rosary that you pray in the cenacle.

3. She will obtain all you need SPIRITUALLY AND THEN MATERIALLY! These days when people are losing their jobs (and soon many more), you will find yourselves having to live on this promise! DO NOT LOOK TO ANYONE OTHER THAN GOD AND OUR LADY for your assistance!

4. SHE WILL BE THE LIGHTNING ROD THAT

DEFLECTS THE CHASTISEMENTS AWAY FROM YOU!!!!

If you do not believe we are in the TIME OF ALL TIMES, then you are not praying enough! Those who are praying can see. So run, do not wait. Get your house in order (the house of your soul). Then Our Lady and the Holy Spirit will lead you to the material preparations you are to do.

Don't believe in material preparations? Read the parable of the ten virgins who went out to get their oil. Five WENT and did something. FIVE DID NOT! The five who did nothing were left out!

Pray, make your peace with your enemies. God wants to work in your lives, but you keep getting in his way. You will not let go of hurts, or unforgiveness, or you just will not give up your sin! God has done all He can to reach you. Now I convey this to you because He wants me to.

IF YOU ARE ALREADY PRAYING, THEN GET EXCITED, AND BE READY. KEEP THE JOY IN YOUR HEART! JESUS IS GOING TO COME BACK SOON! GLORY, GLORY, GLORY!!!!

Visions

SJ: My Dear Brothers and Sisters in Christ:

What follows is an account of the visions that I had during the month of November 1998, and <u>my own personal commentary</u>. Since I was told last Spring that I would receive no more public messages, what has been given to me since then has been visions, and later explanations of the visions by Our Lord and/or Our Lady. This month of November I did receive three visions, but no following explanation. Still, I believe that Our Lord wants me to get them out to you, his holy remnant. I believe that my not receiving an explanation of these three visions is, IN ITSELF, a sign for us.

Visions:
Early in the month of November, during prayer, I had the following vision over a period of time:

I am shown two balls of fire, or something that looks exactly like the picture on the book of messages given to me, "The Great Sign." But I see the two balls coming at each other from opposite directions, and then they meet in the center and collide. I see the illuminated cross in the heavens, then I see a man who is looking up into the heavens. As I have been shown before, I see the explosion of light, and then this man puts his forearm up to his forehead and reels back. He then falls to his knees and begins to cry, holding his hands up to his face.

On November 29, 1998, during a Marian Movement of Priests cenacle, I am shown the following:

I see Jesus, first pointing out to me something up in the heavens. I cannot see what it is. But then he holds up his arm and points for me to see a watch that He is wearing. I KNOW JESUS DOES NOT NEED A WATCH. I look at the watch and both hands are pointing to the 12. He then says to me, "You will not get far into this new year without seeing a great catastrophic event, and many events that have been prophesied, fulfilled." Without my hearing words, but with a kind of infused knowing, I am given the understanding that just as the midnight hour indicates the new year, Jesus is talking about the new CHURCH year that began on that day, which was the First Sunday of Advent.

In the third vision, I am at the bottom of a very long, narrow shaft, or hole. As I am looking upwards I can see a tiny bit of light at what would be the top. I then see someone falling towards me. It is a priest. As he passes different "levels" I see that other people come to the edge, and watch him pass by. Clearly, I know he is going to the bottom of the hole, which would be the "LOWEST" level of purgatory.

I believe that the Lord has clarified for me in the first vision that the Warning of the Soul or the Illumination of Conscience will be accompanied by a great cosmic event that will be 2 heavenly bodies colliding in the heavens.

The vision about the priest gives me a very sad feeling, knowing that this is what is happening to many of our beloved priests who are passing away right now. It also makes me want to re-double my efforts to pray, sacrifice, and fast for them. I know that in the Warning, or Illumination of the Soul, if WE CONTINUE TO PRAY, many will return to the TRUTH! **The priests hold the key for God's people! The more priests that convert and return to the Truth, the better it will be for us in what I**

The Great Sign – Volume II
call, the "grand finale."

My personal comment:

November has been the first month that neither Jesus nor Mary has explained the visions which were given to me. I believe this also is an indication of the impending events. I believe that the Lord has called me to be a sentinel in the watchtower, to ALERT his holy remnant. Even though it may seem to us that nothing is, or will happen, WE MUST NOT BE CAUGHT OFF GUARD! That is exactly what Our Lord says in holy scripture. "Watch ye, therefore, praying AT ALL TIMES, THAT YOU MAY BE ACCOUNTED WORTHY TO ESCAPE ALL THESE THINGS THAT ARE TO COME, AND TO STAND BEFORE THE SON OF MAN." Luke 21:36

Part of Our Lady's Triumph is that this time has been shortened! Again in holy scripture, "And unless those days had been shortened, no flesh should be saved: BUT FOR THE SAKE OF THE ELECT THOSE DAYS SHALL BE SHORTENED." Matthew 24:22

Pray my brothers and sisters, and give thanks to God and Our Lady. Every day that NOTHING happens is ONE DAY LESS that we have to be under the reign of the anti-christ, or in another term, the NEW WORLD ORDER!

I Pray that all of you will be Blessed and truly experience the reality of Jesus in your hearts. I know that the remnant is growing smaller. You are losing perseverance. You are filled with doubts. But I implore you: DO NOT DOUBT! If you and I could see what Our Lord and Lady see, you WOULD believe.

They have spoken often to many persons about these times.

Now we will see. Now we will live THROUGH THE MESSAGES.

We have been and are being put to the test. We must stand in the gap and in prayer, despite what we are feeling. If we only pray when we FEEL like it, or when we FEEL GOOD, then NONE of us will get very far. It doesn't take very long before we know that our feelings don't get us through. Rather, it is our FAITH built on ROCK, on JESUS, on HIS WORD, on HIS TRUTH IN THE TEACHINGS OF HOLY MOTHER CHURCH, TRADITION WITH A CAPITAL "T," and responding to the implorations of Our Lady's messages, that will get us through! If you are not clear about what Our Lady has asked of us, know that it is to get into the state of grace AND STAY THERE!

Please accept my sincere thanks to all of you who are praying for this apostolate and for me, to those of you who are my benefactors, and to those who are spreading the messages. I truly stand in awe of what God is doing, and I do believe we are blessed to live in these times. The time of all times is upon us, but God's Divine Mercy, and Our Lady will get us through.

I don't know if I will receive further explanations of visions, but I do know this: we have been warned, and alerted, and told what to do. If we don't do it, then in the dark days ahead we will surely cry and lament that we SHOULD HAVE PRAYED MORE!

I will keep you all informed as well as I am able. I am united with you in prayer, and I am praying for all of you. Please pray for priests and maybe a little prayer for me too, so that with our Lord's help I can continue to persevere and do the Will of the Father.

Keep the Joy of the Lord in your Hearts! To KNOW JESUS IS TO HAVE JOY!

With such a Mother as Our Mother Mary, who holds us in Her Heart, why do we worry? Through our consecration to the Two Hearts, THEY WILL BE FAITHFUL TO GUIDE, LEAD, AND PROTECT US!

I remain united with you in prayer, and God's servant,

Sadie

The Fire Of My Love! The Fire of My Justice! The Fire Of My Purification

<u>Vision Given to Sadie Jaramillo – December, 1998, and Message Given January 8, 1999</u>

On the morning of Christmas Eve the children and I were coming home to my parents after going to confession. Passing through an intersection, a woman broadsided my car. For me that whole experience demonstrated the power of the angels who protect us. It seemed so surreal, and as we hit, it seemed so gentle. The damage to my car, "gently done" was estimated to be $1300.00, and this woman had no insurance. I turned everything over to Our Lord and Our Lady. I had spoken to the woman's husband and, all along, he assured me that he would fix the car. Everyone else advised me to get a police report and send it to my insurance company. The way of God and the way of the world do not mix very well. However, in prayer I felt that God wanted me to be patient and trust Him to make things happen. I know He gave me that car and that, in reality, it is His to take away. Abandoning myself to prayer, I surrendered all the emotions I wanted to give in to, like frustration, anger, and helplessness. These emotions were ready to take over, had I given in to them, but He came to my aid. I had recently been given a little treasure of a book called, "Trustful Surrender to Divine Providence." That morning in chapel I asked Him to speak to me through this little book. Well, in the way that only God can do, He answered me when I opened the book. It could not have been more profound unless Jesus had made Himself visible, sitting there talking to me. On New Year's Day I received the call to go and pick up my car. The total time my car was gone was two and one half (2 1/2) days!

On December 26, 1998, I attended Holy Mass at the St. Thomas Aquinas College chapel. Before mass began I was alone, venerating some relics that Father Michael had placed alongside the nativity scene. I was talking to Our Lord and Lady as I do, and was presenting to them my requests in prayer. I had told Our Lord that I did not wish to be given any further visions, or hear any further messages. Some of you, my brothers and sisters, will understand what I was saying. I concluded this prayer by saying, "But not my will be done, Lord, yours! If you do want to speak to me, then speak Lord, your servant is listening."

To my surprise, I did begin to hear the voice I have come to recognize as that of Our Lord. After testing and praying I heard the Lord say: "The shedding of your blood will water the seeds of faith for My Church, which will flourish in the Era of Peace." The Lord went on to tell me some personal things concerning my own family, and then left me alone to prepare for mass. As I found the mass prayers and readings for December 26, I was overcome with peace and joy to find that it was the Feast of Saint Stephen, the first martyr of the Church. Our Lord had told me on this very special day that I, too, and many others, would be given the opportunity to shed blood for God and for His Church.

After receiving Holy Communion, while making my thanksgiving, I was shown an explosion of a very large building. It was very similar to the vision that I had been shown before the explosion of the building in Oklahoma City in 1995. However, in this vision I also see men dressed in dark United Nations uniforms holding assault weapons. They assume a stalking posture, like SWAT teams at a crime scene.

Without hearing words, I was given an understanding that another act of this kind of terrorism will come. It will come through the plotting of the higher authorities in our government to continue to prey on the fears of the American people. They will use this to bring an implementation of martial law. Many people will FOOLISHLY welcome this.

Those who pray and understand that the messages of Our Lord and Our Lady are already being fulfilled each day will recognize what is happening.

Message Given to Sadie Jaramillo – January 5, 1999

SJ: Early this morning in prayer, I began to hear the voice I recognize to be that of Our Father saying:

The fire of My Love, the fire of My Justice, the fire of My Purification.

Message Given To Sadie Jaramillo – January 8, 1999, 7:30 a.m.

God our Father gives me the following message:

I AM the Father of Love (Jesus). **My Son and My Spirit give testimony to ME. I WAS, I AM, I WILL ALWAYS BE, and Praises are given to the Trinity!**

My daughter, see what Love your Father in Heaven has tenderly given my creation, in bestowing to it My Only Begotten Son, and pouring upon (humanity) **My Spirit, who purifies and empowers My adopted sons and daughters to accomplish My Will! My Will IS HOLY and desires that ALL should become Holy. I have also given the Queen of Heaven, and Her example of Her "fiat" was given for all to follow.**

I WHO AM THE GREAT I AM, I *AM* APPROACHABLE! With great joy, I lavish (graces and love) **on my children who love Me.**

However, as you look all around my creation, humanity has become pagan again and fallen to levels of degradation never before known! I hear the cries of the faithful and long to gather you all in my arms. You have risen to the call placed on your life and I am well pleased in you. Your cries and prayers I hear and answer. There is no guile in you.

SO NOW TELL MY CHILDREN:
YOU WILL PASS THROUGH THE TRIAL OF FIRE; THE FIRE OF MY LOVE; THE FIRE OF MY JUSTICE; THE FIRE OF MY PURIFICATION!

The Fire of My Love is your illumination of conscience (the Warning)!
The Fire of My Justice will see fire consume the idols of my children.
The Fire of My Purification is the fire that will descend from the heavens to purify and cleanse the earth to prepare for the Time of Peace! It will cover the world with blackness, but those who believe will be prepared (the 3 Days of Darkness)!

Thus, Mankind will be purified! The Church that extends My Life of Grace will be purified! The world will be purified, cleansed from the stench of sin and blood shed of the innocents!

Prayer has been your power and my weakness: for many who have tired and fallen away; for many who have disbelieved; for many who have tried to destroy (projects, discredit authentic apparitions etc.)! **NOW**

The Fire Of My Love! ... My Justice! ... My Purification

WILL THEIR MOMENT OF DECISION COME! THE HOUR OF DECISION IS COME!

The heel that crushes has been formed and you will fight with the Queen, with my angels alongside! You have prayed with others and I have answered through the Queen of Heaven's intercession! You have prayed that My Justice pass quickly over My people, so I have extended The Time of Mercy and shortened the Time of My Wrath!

No longer will my children be left without shepherds to lead (them); **no longer will the Church block the flow of grace; no longer will they betray My Son! The Vicar of My Son** (Pope John Paul II) **will give his immolation with many more to follow!**

<u>**The time of witness to the TRUTH will greatly intensify and increase**</u>**! For this reason, this year will take you to many places where you will speak. My Will is accomplished in you and all that has been spoken of will come to pass. Live every minute of your day aware of My Great Love for you, and in turn LOVE all that are placed before you!**

You are the sentinel (in the watchtower)! **LET THE WORDS GIVEN TO YOU GO FORTH!**

I BLESS YOU, AND I BLESS THOSE WHO BLESS YOU!

SJ: AMEN! PATER NOSTER, AMEN!

God's Great Prodigy Of Love

<u>Message Given to Sadie Jaramillo – January 26, 1999, 3:00 a.m.</u>

SJ: I was awakened hearing words as clearly as if another person were present to me and speaking. They were clear and I could not mistake them as coming from anyone other than the Holy Spirit. As I was thinking about rebuking He answered me: **I AM THE SPIRIT OF THE LIVING GOD AND I PRAISE GOD THE FATHER OF LOVE, AND HIS LOVE** (JESUS) **FOR THEIR GREAT LOVE.**

HOLY SPIRIT: I, the SPIRIT OF THE LIVING GOD have come to tell you the Father of Love has heard the prayers that have risen in His Name! (The novena we have been praying to God the Father.)

In order for you to more fully receive the gifts to be conferred upon you , I ask you for 30 days prayer to Me, The Holy Spirit. The Father of Love prepares to send the FIRE OF HIS LOVE to change forever men's hearts, His Church, your country and the world.

You cannot understand or comprehend this GREAT PRODIGY OF LOVE. (The Warning)

I have come to reassure you and tell you of Gods Great Love for you and all who believe. You who call yourself the "most despised," have touched the Throne of Grace for your great faith.

All these flames of Love (believers who are praying) **have by PRAYER, LIFE AND DEEDS, risen to great degrees**

of Love, so this Trial of Fire will reap the greatest harvest of souls!

There are many who wrestle with God and show little faith. But even these are loved by God.

You cannot understand what comes with your mind, but only with your heart. Do not worry about finances, your father, your family, or any of those things the tempter has been allowed to use against you. (This is for all believers who are going through any kind of trial.)

You have great favor with God for this: your littleness before Him in prayer.

All that has been asked of you will be accomplished. Thus, the preparation must be made through these 30 Days of Prayer.

Do not fear anything you see, or hear, for this comes to the world as part of the Trial of Fire proclaimed to you by the Father of Love. Though this is being asked of you, you may share this request with others.

Those who have faithfully prayed to the Father have etched themselves in His Heart never to be erased, for He is a Loving Father eager to show Love to those who come to Him in prayer. (Again, this is for those who are praying wholeheartedly and have converted totally in their hearts.)

Again, I tell you, you cannot comprehend what comes!

Great changes for the Body of Christ, (and for) the world!

I breathe on you and whisper to you the secrets of God; I fill you with HIS LOVE and obtain blessings (for you and all who believe)**!**

SJ: AMEN.

SJ: My response was to pray the following:

"Praise to You Father, My Love, and Spirit Most Holy!"

I then stayed up to pray the Chaplet of Mercy and the Rosary to God the Father.

Note to this message:

I believe with all my heart that the Holy Spirit wants us to be as ready as possible for the great outpouring of grace in the Warning. This is why He has come to ask me to pray 30 days to Him. I am starting these 30 days of prayer today, the Feast of St. Thomas of Aquinas. I am including a copy of the prayer I was given several years ago, by a beloved priest friend of all of ours. I invite all of you to start whenever you receive notice of this, and begin your own personal 30 days of prayer to the Holy Spirit.

May we all see very soon the fulfillment of the promises of Our Lady and Our Lord. THE TRIUMPH OF THE TWO HEARTS, AND THE ERA OF PEACE!

You can e-mail me at sorrowfulr@fathersvictory.org. Alternatively, visit our website at www.fathersvictory.org. I try to be available for you, so please do not hesitate to write to 401 Garnet Way, Santa Maria, CA 93454, or call at (805) 928-3994.

I encourage all of you to remain expectant and joyful! We

are living in a most wonderful and awesome time. A time for all of us to respond to the Holy Father's invitation to be the apostles of these latter days, and be ready to evangelize! As always I remain united with you in prayer.

Sadie J.

CONSECRATION TO THE HOLY SPIRIT FOR UNIVERSAL SANCTIFICATION

O my Holy Spirit, perennial font of grace and love, Joy of the Trinity, Creator of the universe, sweetest guest of hearts, light and splendor of souls, I, (N.N.) the lowliest of the sinners to you I come, with humility and confidence and dare to consecrate myself to you.

O Divine Spirit, breathe on my weak and sterile being and bring me the light, the warmth and the abundance of holy works. Come to my soul to purify everything which is defective and sinful. Adorn my soul with the immensity of your richness, the power of your gift and the fire of your love. Make my soul your perpetual and sweet Dwelling Place, and a magnificent temple of your Glory.

O my Divine Spirit, furnace of eternal love for souls, in your infinite bounty and charity, you search for the heart of men to give them a new divine life. You want to renew the world with your perennial Pentecost of graces virtues and gifts. This is the time that souls, more than ever, need your presence, your grace and your power to be detached from sinful ways and to be brought to the ideals of the Gospel and to the imitation of Divine Perfection. Today, I come to you, I consecrate myself to you, and I open myself to your mysterious and divine work, to be completely renewed in body and soul so that I can become a worthy vessel of your bounty and election.

O my Holy Spirit, I believe with all my Heart in your divine love for all the faithful and especially I believe in your love for me. I feel that you have called me, that you knocked at the door of my heart, that you are with me that you fill me with your love and tenderness. Therefore, I want to be yours. I want to belong to you and dedicate myself to you and to your work forever. Grant that I might know and experience the splendor of your light, the gleam of your flames, the richness of your Grace, the marvels of your omnipotence. Show to me and to all the souls, the face of your Love and the depth of your Divinity, so that my soul and the souls of my brothers might be subdued by the charm of the inexpressible beauty of your Divine Majesty.

O my Divine Spirit, I am yours. Take complete possession of all my being. With all my love, with all my joy, with all the might of my heart I consecrate myself to your divine love, to your sweet bounty.

O my Holy Spirit, in my loneliness please be to me like a mother, like a friend, like a guide, like an advocate. I will be all yours! I will love you with the simplicity of a child and with the ardor of a seraphim.

O my Eternal Love, I want to know you, and I want to love you. I want to preach about you, I want to bring you to the souls and the souls to you.

O my Divine Spirit, I love you and I consecrate myself to you, but I have a great fear! I fear of not being faithful to you, of not persevering in your love. I fear that I will be attracted by the things of this world and by the creatures of this world. I strongly fear not to keep my promises and even not to live this, my consecration to you.

O my Love, please, I beg you not to abandon me for my infidelity, for my weakness for my misery. Never do I want to be separated from you; nothing will let me be far from you. I want to be yours forever. Please help me to overcome all my interior and exterior difficulties. I especially, consecrate and recommend to you this my heart, subject to all the waves of this earthly life.

O my Holy Spirit, this consecration is like a personal convenant with you. I offer and consecrate myself to you and I beg you to grant me this favor. Confirm me in your Grace, in your Love, in your Work. Be my joy, my consolation, my strength, my rest and my all. In spite of my nothingness, I desire to be your devout servant, your faithful friend. Grant me to be your Apostle, the Apostle of your infinite love, of your infinite tenderness for souls. Grant me to be an Apostle of universal sanctification.

CONCLUDING PRAYER

O my Holy Spirit, in all my weaknesses and infirmities, help me always with your grace and win me always with the kiss of your eternal love. Transport me always in the kingdom of truth and charity. Bring me and unite me continuously to Jesus Christ and the Eternal Father.

AMEN.

PRAYER TO OBTAIN THE HOLY SPIRIT

I.

Eternal Father, In the Name of Jesus Christ, and through the merits of the Immaculate Virgin Mary, send me the Holy Spirit.

Come, O Holy Spirit, into my heart and sanctify it. Come, O Father of the Poor, and lift me up.
Come, O Author of all good, and console me.
Come, O Light of the minds, and enlighten me.
Come, O Consoler of the Souls and comfort me.
Come, O sweet Guest of hearts, and do not depart from me.
Come, O real Refresher of my life, and restore me.

Glory Be To The Father
(3 times)

Holy Spirit, Eternal Love come to me with your ardors. Come, and inflame our hearts.

II.

Eternal Father, In the Name of Jesus Christ, and through the merits of the Immaculate Virgin Mary, send me the Holy Spirit.

Holy Spirit, God of infinite charity, give me Your holy Love.
Holy Spirit, God of virtue, convert me.
Holy Spirit, Fount of celestial illumination, dissipate my ignorance.
Holy Spirit, Author of true peace, repose in my heart.
Holy Spirit, God of infinite purity, sanctify my soul.
Holy Spirit God of all happiness, communicate yourself to my heart.
Holy Spirit, substantial Love of the Father of the Son, dwell with us.

Glory Be To The Father
(3 times)

Holy Spirit, Eternal Love, come to me with your ardors. Come, and inflame our hearts.

III.

Eternal Father, in the Name of Jesus Christ, and through the merits of the Immaculate Virgin Mary, send me the Holy Spirit.
Come, Holy Spirit, and give me the gift of Wisdom
Come, Holy Spirit, and give me the gift of Understanding
Come Holy Spirit and give me the gift of Counsel
Come Holy Spirit, and give me the gift of Fortitude
Come Holy Spirit and give me the gift of Knowledge
Come Holy Spirit and give me the gift of Piety
Come Holy Spirit and give me the gift of the Holy Fear of God.

Glory Be To The Father
(3 times)

Holy Spirit, Eternal Love, come to me with your ardors. Come and inflame our hearts.

IV.

Come, Holy Spirit, to fill my soul with your gifts. Then, I will repent of my faults. I will take to heart the mortification and the detachment from all things of the earth that are vain, useless, and delusive.
Spirit consoler, I am poor, I am naked, and deprived of your gifts. You alone are the Most Sweet Guest of my soul, the refresher in my pains, the control of my passions, the solace in my affliction. O Most Blessed Light, please penetrate the innermost part of my heart, without Your help I will always be empty of everything. I will always be wicked.

O Celestial Spirit, come and wash my sordidness, take away the sterility of my heart, and cure the wounds of my soul.

O Divine Love, warm my coldness, lower my haughtiness, restore me and guide me in the path of the blessed eternity.

And finally, distribute, O Holy Spirit, to me and to all the faithful who pray to you and who confide in you, your seven celestial gifts, so that with them all of us will reach one day the happy attainment of our salvation, the reward of our virtues, and the joy of eternal life.

The Great Sign – Volume II

Amen.

OBJECTIVES OF THE CONSECRATION

1. To live and grow in the grace of God everyday.
2. To know the value and the marvels of the grace.
3. To spread the knowledge and the devotion of the Holy Spirit.
4. To realize the presence of the Holy Spirit in ourselves since we are Temples of the Holy Spirit.
5. To repeat frequently acts of faith and love to the Holy Spirit.
6. To supplicate the Holy Spirit for the conversion of sinners.
7. To pray the Holy Spirit to shower all His graces and gifts upon the universal church.
8. To ask the Holy Spirit for all His Gifts as a continual personal Pentecost.
9. To open our soul to the faithfulness to the inspirations of the Holy Spirit.
10. To be a tireless worker for the sanctification of oneself and of others.

Nihil Obstat: Reverend Monsignor Joseph C. Downing, Censor Deputatus
Imprimatur: Most Reverend George H. Guilfoyle, DD. J.D.
Bishop of Camden,
December 24, 1975

Copies of this prayer can be obtained from:

THE REV. THOMAS M. ADINOLFI

Vocationist Fathers
644 E. End Ave.
Lancaster, PA 17604
(717) 392-4118

The Fulfillment Of Calvary Comes To Humanity!

Messages to Sadie Jaramillo – March 11, 1999, 10:00 a.m.

Visions to Sadie Jaramillo:

At various times throughout this last month I have been shown the following visions. Today I am instructed to write what I have been shown.

First, I am shown four horses. Their riders are not distinguishable by me. One horse is white, one red, one black, and one is a color I cannot make out, but is rather pale. Then Our Lord directed me to The Book of Revelation, Chapter 6. Therein lies the meaning of these horses.

I am also shown 7 angels holding bowls. In these bowls, I see something that looks to me like red-hot charcoal. I am reminded of a vision that was shown to me February 3, 1993. I was shown these same seven angels and I KNOW that what they hold is the Justice of God. Read Revelation 15:1-8.

I am also shown a heart that I recognize to be the Sacred Heart of Jesus. From this Sacred Heart comes forth a cross and Jesus is hanging on the Cross.

I am also shown Jesus on the Cross at Calvary, with an ocean of people gathered at its foot. Jesus is also standing to the left of the Cross and pointing His arm to direct me to gaze at this vision, as if He wanted me to see this mass of people extending as far as I could see.

I would also like to share that I have been going through a particularly difficult time in my prayer life, a time that seems to me so dry. I do not feel anything when I pray, but I pray because I KNOW it is what God wants me to do. I share this, for I would like you to know that this comes to all of us. Many who have gone on before us struggled in this same way. Please do not give up. Please continue to pray. That is all I can share. Persevere! This is a VIRTUE.

Message to Sadie Jaramillo, March 11, 1999, – 10:00 a.m.

I test and rebuke what I begin to hear. Our Lord answers me as follows:

JESUS: Daughter of My Sacred Heart, I WHO AM, PRAISE THE FATHER AND THE SPIRIT, AND I WHO AM, RECEIVE THE PRAISES OF MY PEOPLE!

My mother's little sorrowful rose, my Mother who is the Mother of Mercy, now extends to humanity this time of Mercy. We (The Trinity) **have not refused Her constant requests for Mercy. What I tell you now, I ask you to convey to my body** (of believers):

BECAUSE YOU HAVE PRAYED, Mercy has been extended!

BECAUSE YOU HAVE PRAYED, Justice has been shortened!

BECAUSE YOU HAVE PRAYED, souls loved by Me, but destined for hell have been saved!

BECAUSE YOU HAVE PRAYED, my signs are given to the body, and are recognizable to THOSE WHO ARE PRAYING!

BECAUSE YOU HAVE PRAYED, SECRETS WILL BE REVEALED, SECRETS WILL BE COMPLETED!

BECAUSE YOU HAVE PRAYED, my brothers (the priests) **though they should be condemned, will be saved!**

BECAUSE YOU HAVE PRAYED, my Vicar, JOHN PAUL II is strengthened to fulfill the Divine Will of God!

I say to my body now: I will invade the interior of your heart and soul, just as I kept in the interior of My Sacred Heart the knowledge and sorrow of the ultimate purpose of my Life: to be born of a Woman, to live in poverty and humility, and fulfill the LOVE OF THE FATHER; to suffer and die for a humanity that would not all accept this great sacrifice of Love! I held this in My Sacred Heart and this caused me the greatest anguish. THE FULFILLMENT OF CALVARY COMES TO HUMANITY! DIVINELY, HUMANITY SHALL SEE, AND LAMENT OVER WHAT THEY SHALL SEE!

My Mother, who is the Mother of Mercy, weeps for this time to come to humanity. As a TRUE MOTHER OF LOVE she, united to the sorrows of my Soul, desires the salvation of all her children.

Many times over you have been told of that which is to come. See what I have shown you in the fields of the harvest! They are ripe for the reaping! And I will bring to life those who have been dead in their sins. I will bring life, fervor, and the fire of my Love to those who love me now. Together, we will work and labor in this field of souls. The holy and just wrath of God your Father and my Father, comes to purify for his Time. The

Spirit comes to fill, again, the body with the gifts of his Love. NOT ONE SOUL WILL BE LEFT WITHOUT RECOURSE TO MY MERCY! What they choose to do, is left to their free wills. But because you have prayed, many that would have still rejected Me will be saved! This is a great gift! Your tears, your sufferings, bodily and emotional, have been gathered tenderly by your Mother. Daily She presents them to the Father of Love. Daily her requests are answered.

Because the time for the enemy to rear his power and ugly head has come, now divinely, remember my children that it is the Power of God that will triumph! You will see the Era of Peace come through the Triumph of the Two Hearts! That which has been shown to you is the fulfillment of many prophecies given not only to you, but also to many of my instruments risen all around the world. The idols of man shall, in an instant, come crashing down!

That which man has created for deception will be caused to be seen by the many who will receive the grace of LIGHT. I AM LIGHT. I AM TRUTH. I AM THE WAY, WHICH YOU SHOULD FOLLOW!

Cosmic blows to the earth come! Hearts will faint for what they shall see! But those who pass through my Fire will be strong, and (fulfill) the purpose of my Heart, Sacred, and Broken: my Spouse, THE CHURCH! Enemies will be defeated! Splendor will be restored, and indeed surpassed!

Mankind will be reconciled and restored to the Author of Life: God the Father! Through the Eucharistic Reign of my Sacred Heart, the Spirit will bestow His gifts to the hearts of mankind! Peace will be restored! God's

WILL, will be done here on the Earth as it has always been done in Heaven!

Draw close to this Sacred Heart!
Do not fear what you shall soon see! I AM with you! Kings and Princes, Leaders of Nations, they will see the folly of their plans!

Give this message of Love to my people.

Yes, you wonder at the less frequent receiving of these messages. I tell you: The silence in Heaven is over, and now you my people will pass through the great trial. My instruments are silenced, and words spoken long ago come to pass. What I will show you in the days ahead will help you to help others. Though you will not be able to distribute them as you have done up to now, the purpose of your call and mission will be fulfilled. You know what this means. I am with you unto the end.

For the other projects, have not you been told obstacles would be removed, and hearts would be touched? Your prayers have reached the throne of Grace! And this too will rise, here and in many other places. My children will be greatly consoled, and graces will be received. Continue as you have. This will move in a way that is swift and complete!

(Our Lord refers here to the Cross of Peace Apostolate in Santa Maria, which I had been wondering whether He would address. He also addressed my thoughts about the messages coming less and less frequently. This cross is a material cross made out of Purple Heart wood. But there will be illuminated crosses that will rise in other parts of the world that will interiorly call many people to gather there to get through this difficult time).

My sentinel let my words go forth! With my Mother, I bless you and all who believe!

SJ: AMEN! AVE MARIA!

Behold The Time Draws Near

Visions and Messages to Sadie Jaramillo – April 24 to May 21, 1999

My dear brothers and sisters in the Lord Jesus Christ:

I greet you all in the name of Our Savior Jesus Christ and of His Mother, Mary, Queen and Advocate of all Graces!

What follows is an account of the last five or six weeks. From April 23 through the 30, I took the children and spoke to Canadian groups in Saskatoon, Dysart, Zenon Park, and Prince Albert. Then we made a pilgrimage with friends in Jesus and Mary to Garabandal and Lourdes from May 4 to 21, returning in time to attend the Eucharistic Conference, May 22 and 23, in Paso Robles, California. What a whirlwind of activity! I pray now that the Holy Spirit will enlighten me to share accurately with you what I saw and heard.

April 24, 1999, SASKATOON: I am tremendously blessed to have the opportunity to speak in the Church of the Canadian Martyrs. Father Maurice, so gracious in opening the doors of his parish, offers the Holy Sacrifice of the Mass after we pray the Rosary. Unbeknownst to me, a Ukrainian Rite Catholic Bishop, Basil Filevich, is present and listening. After the talk, and a question and answer period, Bishop Basil makes a very kind statement for which I give Praise, Honor and Glory to God, and His Queen, Our Mother Mary! Sunday, April 25, I speak again at the Church of the Canadian Martyrs, and then am driven to the town of Dysart and welcomed by the Catholic community.

April 26, DYSART: In the morning I experience a demonic attack. The demon holds a black skull filled with blood and tries to reach me. Praise God, Our Lady had shown me the power of rebuking satan in the name of Jesus! The rest of that morning and afternoon my head feels like it will explode. The suffering was intense, and I didn't feel I would be able to speak that evening. As I lay in pain and prayer, I offered it up for Our Lord's and Our Lady's intentions, but especially for priests. It was during this time that, as C. played "Ave Maria" on the piano, Mother Mary appeared as Our Lady of the Miraculous Medal. In the vision she lifts a crown of thorns from my head, and replaces it with a crown of roses. As has happened before, I fell asleep, and when I awoke the pain had been lifted so that I could give the talk as scheduled. Praise be to Jesus and Mary! Most of the people in attendance were not from the town, but had driven some distance to be there. The following morning my hosts drive me halfway to the next town, Zenon Park.

April 27, ZENON PARK: Father Charles Charest picks me up and once in Zenon Park, opens his parish, Our Lady of the Nativity, where I speak once in the afternoon, and again later that evening. Father leaves me with my hosts for that particular evening. Next day Father Charest drives me halfway to Prince Albert, or PA as they say in Canada.

April 28, PRINCE ALBERT: Again, I am graciously hosted, and in the evening speak to the Catholic community at the Thrift Lodge. I meet Msgr. Leblanc after the talk, and then am met by the hosts who will drive me back to Saskatoon.

April 29, 1999, SASKATOON: In preparation for my talk later that evening at the Knights of Columbus Hall, I attend Holy Mass at the Cathedral of St. Paul. It is there that I experience a word from the Lord and see a vision. Over this celebrant's head I can see a cross as he celebrates Holy Mass. This priest reveals his great reverence in offering up this most awesome miracle, especially when he pronounces the words that consecrate the host to become JESUS! During my thanksgiving, after receiving Holy Communion, I hear the Lord, and I test.

JESUS: See this beloved brother of mine, how greatly I am consoled and loved by him. So few are they (PRIESTS) **who console my wounded heart.**

At the end of Holy Mass we stay to pray the Rosary. During the fourth decade of the Joyful Mysteries, I begin to see the following vision. I tested and this is what followed:

JESUS: I AM THE GREAT SHEPHERD. You know my voice, my sheep follow Me! Praises are sung to the GREAT I AM!

VISION: I see Jesus walking some distance before me, and he is walking very fast. His hair is blowing in the wind because of the speed of His walk. I am following Him and by my peripheral vision I can see that there are others walking to the sides of me and behind me. Then He quickly stops and turns and looks directly at me and is pointing to me. He then turns and points to the heavens and in the sky there is an illuminated cross. To the left of the cross there is a clock. Both hands are at the twelve o'clock hour.

Jesus says to me:

JESUS: Behold the time draws near! Behold the time draws near! Behold the time draws near! I have come to ask you to tell my children: "I come to say to those who are strong, BE STRONGER STILL and to those who are weak, BE STRONG IN ME!"

The vision ends. But it was very profound. It left me quite breathless.

<u>Garabandal, Spain</u>: Next day, Friday, April 30, we say our good-byes to the wonderful people who hosted us and return to Santa Maria, California to repack for the pilgrimage to Garabandal, Spain. On Monday morning, May 4, we begin the long grueling flight from Los Angeles to Madrid. We reach Garabandal by a picturesque six-hour drive into the Cantabrian Mountains of northern Spain. In preparation for this very special pilgrimage I began a Rosary novena that I entrusted to Padre Pio to honor his beatification on May 2. My novena was to end on the Feast of the Ascension, May 13. Since we were staying at an inn near Saint Sebastian Church in Garabandal, we could see numerous groups of pilgrims arriving, some accompanied by priests. We were graced to attend the Holy Mass, and exposition, adoration and Benediction of the Blessed Sacrament celebrated by these pilgrim priests with extraordinary fervor and reverence. Oh how wonderful God is! I felt like a sponge trying to absorb all that God provided for me there.

During my stay at the inn, I helped translate for some of the pilgrims in the religious articles store, which was downstairs. It was there that I had the privilege to meet some of the religious who are in new orders. If I can say anything, it is that GOD IS WORKING AND MOVING IN THE HEARTS OF THE RELIGIOUS WHO ARE BEING RAISED UP TO TAKE THE CHURCH OVER THE THRESHOLD, INTO THE NEW ERA! These are religious who love Our Lord and Our Lady, and who truly believe in the REAL PRESENCE of Jesus in the Blessed Sacrament! I saw that the more this truth is denied, the more God works by means of your and my prayers, sufferings, trials, and sacrifices!

On the day I completed my novena, I had the grace to be blessed by a wonderful pilgrim priest. At the age of 16 he had been told by Padre Pio that he would be a priest. He had a stole that had belonged to Padre Pio and as he blessed me I smelled a most wonderful fragrance! I thought, "Can I receive any more graces?" Later that evening, as I was in prayer, the phrase came to me, "Can you not watch just one hour with Me?" So I planned on joining others in a prayer vigil for the Feast of the Ascension up in the pines above the village. That was where our Blessed Mother had appeared so many times to the children (Conchita, Jacinta, Mary Loli and Mary Cruz) between 1961 and 1965. I had planned on being there from midnight until three o'clock in the morning. Once at the pines, my children fell asleep. It became damper and colder, so when a couple went down at 2 o'clock in the morning, I took the children down and prayed the last hour in our room. But a wonderful nun, Sister Bernadette, gave us all a wonderful witness by consoling Christ there from about 8:30 p.m. Wednesday evening until 6:00 a.m. Ascension Thursday morning!

May 13, Feast of the Ascension, GARABANDAL: For the Feast of the Ascension, Bishop Roman Danylak, a Ukrainian Rite Catholic bishop, was offering the Holy Mass with four concelebrating priests, and it was wonderful! Again I asked, "What more can you give me Lord?" Thursday evening we went up to the pines and joined many people from all over the world, including a group from the Franciscan University of Steubenville, Ohio. It was just wonderful. As we were in the pines praying the Rosary about 8:30 p.m., there was suddenly thunder! This was not ordinary thunder, but like thunder that might have accompanied God's conversations with Moses! To the right of us there was a cloud of fog or smoke, or something that looked like that, rolling toward us until it reached a certain point and rolled back, all the while accompanied by thunder. Some others who were there also saw the cloud and heard the thunder. This was not a private vision! We were in the presence of God and Our Lady, and we received a multitude of graces. Over and over I heard from the others who were there that they had not intended to go to Garabandal. Just like me, many of the other pilgrims felt like they had been called there.

Friday, May 14, LOURDES: We left next day in the early morning drizzle on an unplanned trip to Lourdes. It turned out wonderfully, even though our bus driver missed a turn and it took us an additional six hours to get to Lourdes! All of us were so engrossed in prayer and conversation that we hardly noticed, and were content to offer it up. At Lourdes we saw many of the same people who had been in Garabandal. I attended Holy Mass in the side Chapel of St. Michael the Archangel, in which he is honored by a magnificent statue. St. Michael the Archangel is Guardian of Holy Mother Church and we call on him, as well as our Guardian Angels, to protect us!

May 18, GARABANDAL: Four days later, after returning to Garabandal, I began to receive the following message. I was in the religious articles store below our room admiring a statue of Christ the Redeemer, with His hands bound, that is known to the Trinitarians, of which I am a member of the Third Order. It moved me and I prayed in my heart: "Lord, it is beautiful, I want it. I don't have to have it, but I want it. But your will be done." I then went upstairs to our room and after a little while felt led to go back downstairs and buy it. About noon, after returning to our room with the statue, I began to hear the voice of the Blessed Mother. As always, I test and rebuke in the Name of Jesus. I am answered as follows:

MARY: I, my little sorrowful rose, am your Mother of Sorrows, giving the world flesh of my flesh, the Only Begotten of God, the Word made flesh: JESUS! Lift up your hearts and heads, My Son comes in Glory! The songs of praise rise incessantly to the Glory of the Trinity! I address your thoughts in regard to the infrequent timing now of my words to you.

Through your mission you reach many who, from the beginning (of your mission), **I told you I would bring to you. Thus I announce to you: The grave events foretold loom on the horizon and the hour of decision is come! My sorrows are consoled in the hearts of those who live my words of request to humanity! To you and to many others who live this Love, have been given many graces needed for the days ahead.**

I bring you here to meet and know those whom have been put in your path. (Our Lady speaks here of the people, priests and bishop I met while in Garabandal.) **You my children must lift one another in prayer, for the trial of suffering increases to the point of indescribable heights. The hour of God's Justice arrives for humanity. I encourage one and all to hold fast to the Two Hearts, for there you will find guidance and protection. The Glory of the Lord will visit his people. Those who stand steadfast and firm hold onto this hope. I leave you now, for my Son will speak to you.**

JESUS: Daughter of my Father's Love! I AM your Love! This I tell you to say to your director: "In this statue, you see once again they have bound my hands. Through your consecrated hands and love you must work to renew the Church of my Sacred Heart! Did I not shed every drop of blood? And did not every drop of water flow from my wounded Heart for this Love to be

bestowed to humanity? I do not ask for conformity. I ask for the Spirit of Love to renew my Church."

This ignorant child of God's has been taken from the darkness into my light. I have used her heart and her tears, her fiat to save many of your brothers and mine. Now I ask you, into whose heart you have bid me to enter, "renew my Church, not to conformity, but to heights of sacredness long forgotten!"

If you give me your acquiescence, my Spirit, my power, will move through you and I will bless your work and efforts. But as to suffering? I ask you to bind your suffering to My Heart that your suffering will be lost in Mine. There is a New Age dawning and the Fire of Purification will rage as a fire ignited from one end of the Earth to the other! It is the New Era I call you to prepare for, wherein holiness will rise and flourish to heights long forgotten. Search My Heart and My Spirit will light the way! There is a foundation already laid. I wait for your answer.

Do not fear for My Mother and I will walk with you. I want all to see my ministers called to service and a life of holiness. Unbind my hands, to live a life of service through your hands. My enemies, it would seem, appear to have triumphed, for my sacramental love is being subverted and kept from my people. Unbind my hands! Let Me live through the indelible sign of your vocation. **Read this book** (To My Priests by Concepcion Cabrera De Armida) **and I will unlock the desires of My Sacred Heart! Unbind My hands!** (Here Our Lord leads me to holy scripture: "Let a man so account of us, as of the ministers of Christ, and the dispensers of the mysteries of God." 1 Cor. 4:1, Duoay-Rheims)

In My Heart I have placed your heart and My Mother. She who is Advocate of mankind, Co-redeemer with Me, Treasurer and Mediatrix of all graces will freely dispense the graces needed here.

Our Lord continues to me:

JESUS: Did you hear the thunder and see the appearance of a cloud coming towards all up at the pines (in Garabandal)? In the inner heart of those living intimately with the Two Hearts the thunder of God's Justice was heard. And the Glory of God will fall and be left as a sign for all who live that God has spoken and delivered up to His Justice those who would not listen. In this time of retreat into my Love you are going to return to work still in My harvest. Many more will come to all places of Holy sites, for as the signs of confusion rise some will know their hour of decision and retreat to Holy places. You have stood in the company of future saints and martyrs. Thus you see that I who AM, will that my Mother be recognized and be given the fullness of God's power through the proclamation of the dogma. You will see it, and with it will come the hour of darkness in the sanctuaries of the church. Describe your vision.

VISION: At various times during my stay in Garabandal, I have been shown in a vision the sanctuary light in a church go out. The sanctuary remains dark. Now go, prepare your heart for the reception of your creator. More will be given later. (At this point I leave to prepare for Holy Mass.) Here the message in Garabandal ends.

<u>May 21, RETURNING HOME</u>: On the way home, as I am praying on the plane, I hear Jesus speak to me. I test and receive the following message:

JESUS: You will not be home a fortnight before prophesied events begin to be realized. Now, I tell you my daughter, that what comes for humanity will be accomplished for the greater Glory of God through the hearts of the little and the lowly. That the time of all times is upon mankind, but they have eyes and do not see, and ears and do not hear. For they have stony hearts and will not open their hearts to the lover of their soul and their Savior. Stiff necked are my people, but the greater sin falls to my shepherds who have neither believed, nor converted. Few are they, and mind you, I do know who they are, who try by their actions to show their love for Me. Woe to you, who are neither saved nor allow others to be saved! Woe to you! You will stand in judgement and then you will tremble and know the Truth, that now you deny! Woe to you! This is why I walk swiftly now, to show you that the time of Mercy ends and Justice begins! Many have anxiously waited for new words and they do not understand that all that needs to be said has been said. Now the living out and the fulfillment of our words will come swiftly to pass. Be encouraged and joyful, for if you are bound to the Two Hearts you will know peace in chaos, joy through sorrows, courage in time of terror. In all you will feel the presence of My Mother and Myself, whose love knows no bounds! I who AM the Lover of souls, call you still, to work in this harvest. Your strength will be my strength, your words will be my words, until I call you to my bosom! Tell my children: 'Do not fear!' I come swiftly to establish a new era, a new reign through my Eucharistic Heart and the Immaculate Heart of Mary, My Mother! Pray still for my brothers the priests! They do not know what awaits them. Peace my daughter, to you and to all who believe.

SJ: AMEN. AMEN. AMEN.

Be Not Afraid!

Message to Sadie Jaramillo – August 1, 1999, 3:00 a.m. – Feast of St. Alphonsus Ligouri

I am awakened with a severe headache. As I lay in bed offering up the pain and trying to pray, I begin to see a vision. In this vision I see a ball of fire with a tail. I see it hit a surface. I have been shown this ball of fire before. But always it is hurtling through the darkness of space. This time I see it HIT a surface. I DO NOT know what this surface is. With impact there is an explosion and a tremendous light. I understand these to be the cosmic signs that will accompany the illumination of conscience.

Then as I continue to lie there I begin to hear Our Lady asking me to write. I test what I am beginning to hear according to scripture.

Our Lady answers as follows:

MARY: My daughter, my little sorrowful rose, I am the Queen of Heaven, the Woman clothed with the stars, the moon at my feet and brighter than the noonday Sun! (Our Lady refers to herself in Her image of Our Lady of Guadalupe, to whom I often pray. She expresses the theme of the Catena Legionis antiphon: 'Who is she that cometh forth as the morning rising, fair as the Moon, bright as the Sun, terrible as an army set in battle array?') **To me was given the grace of conceiving Immaculately the Incarnate Son of God!**[1] **Praise God the Father for this Great Love! My child what do you see?**

SJ: Our Lady refers here to the vision described above, and to three other visions that have come to me during the months of June/July.

The first of these occurred on June 10, when Father P. called me from Rome. As he prayed with me I was shown a vision. This does not always happen, but today it was a very beautiful vision.

I saw an image of the world, and hovering over it, an image of the Holy Spirit as a dove. Above Him was an image of God the Father. It was like the image of God the Father that is on my website.

Our Lord is below the Father's right hand, beside the world, and Our Lady is below his left side.

Suddenly the world explodes in fire. It becomes one ball of fire.

I have received no message or words other than the understanding given.

The Fire of the Holy Spirit will burn and change the hearts of those who are OPEN to His Holy Work. In His message of January 8, 1999, Jesus had said we would pass through the Fire of God's Love, the Fire of God's Justice and the Fire of God's Purification. All of these have to do with fire.

As the darkness descends God will use the hearts of mankind that do not stifle the works of the Holy Spirit. Yes, not all will accept. But many will. I pray that we all will allow the Holy Spirit to move us. But we cannot move in what we do not know. Please pray, read Holy Scripture and the teachings of Holy Mother Church. We must all be grounded on the ROCK!

The second vision was given at various times during the

months of June and July during prayer and Holy Mass. In the vision I see a bolt of lightning. I call it lightning, but I have never seen lightning like this. It was WIDE and striking repeatedly. I also see the Resurrected Jesus over to the side and He points to the heavens. There in the heavens is the illuminated cross. As I am gazing at it, the Corpus of Jesus appears on the Cross. This vision also refers to the illumination of conscience.

The third vision was first given during one of the prayer cenacles, and was repeated at other times during private prayer. In this vision I see Jesus sitting in a confessional behind a screen. I can see the shadow of someone on the other side of the screen. Jesus is looking at me very INTENTLY. His gaze is loving, but serious. He is holding his fingers and hand up giving absolution. Jesus does not speak aloud, but I am given this understanding: "Tell them ALL to go to confession."

MARY: On this morning I greet you with great love and motherly tenderness as you remember our first conversation seven years ago. This day brings you great graces and blessings. You have seen the hunger in the faces of my children and their hearts will burn with the words spoken by you, but given by the Holy Spirit. My Beloved Spouse brings great conviction to His Words!

The signs spoken of over and over to you are even now in the process of becoming a reality. Yes, I have striven to shorten this great time of the bloody persecution. I have striven to bring all God's children home to the Father, home to the Mercy of My Son Jesus, whose Heart is so full of Love and compassion.

Those who are prepared, let them take heed.

BE NOT AFRAID! I take you into my Immaculate Heart, Garden of God's Love. I, to whom has been given the task of bringing satan under my heel, come to reassure with these words.

The heavens will flash with the brightness of light that will bring fear and terror to some! Others, well prepared, will pass into the greatest work of love. For this daughter of mine (the Church), so loved by Me and so wounded, will be eclipsed. For a moment it will seem as though the enemies of God will triumph and reign. But true to HIS WORD, "the gates of hell shall NOT prevail!"

This for my children continues to be the greatest sign (indicating the coming) **of impending events.**

My Son, who absolves and forgives through His brother priests, waits tenderly for His flock to return!

The blows of the Father's Justice will resound in the heavens. It will seem as though the very stars are shaken from their place! Just as you heard in the thunder at Garabandal, so will you know the very voice of God speaking to your heart announcing to you the great prodigious event.

TELL MY CHILDREN: "Do not let the blows of God's Mercy (in His Justice) **catch you unaware! Do not let the lack of faith fulfill scripture in you! Do not let the Coming of my Son, Jesus, like the thief in the night, bring terror to your heart! Oh Great and terrible is the Day of the Lord! Only those who allow the Spirit of God to speak to their hearts and whisper the secrets of God; only those who approach the Father with the simplicity of a child** (will be ready). **A child goes asking, KNOW-**

ING he will not be turned away. You are the ones called now to ready yourselves for this Battle of Love for the souls Jesus, My Son, yearns for! Keep His Peace in your hearts. DO NOT allow your hearts to be troubled! The Father of Love permits not one thing to harm you, but all things to strengthen you."

As the Magi looked to the heavens and found the announcement of the birth of the Messiah, so too now! Look to the heavens, for they announce to you the Second Coming of My Son, Jesus, in Glory! Be not afraid, my daughter, tell my children: "BE NOT AFRAID!"

On this day I bless you with the great love of Your Mother!

SJ: AMEN!

---

[1]. **Editor's Note:** Since God's indwelling in Jesus as Man is for our redemption, and His indwelling in Mary is for her as the Mother of the Redeemer, God must have dwelt in Jesus and Mary from the very first moment of their existence. By overshadowing the virgin Mary the Holy Spirit espoused her and she was given the grace of conceiving immaculately the Incarnate Son of God without the ministry of man. Luke 1:35-36. St. Methodius celebrates Mary's divine espousal in his Banquet of the Ten Virgins, Discourse XI, Chapter II: "The parent of Thy life, that unspotted Grace and undefiled Virgin, bearing in her womb without the ministry of man, by an immaculate conception, and who thus became suspected of having betrayed the marriage-bed, she, O blessed One, when pregnant, thus spoke: 'I keep myself pure for Thee, O Bridegroom, and holding a lighted torch I go to meet Thee.'"   Roberts, Alexander and Donaldson, James, Anti-Nicene Fathers: Vol. VI, (Oak Harbor, WA: Logos Research Systems, Inc.) 1997

I AM with you to the end! Be not afraid!

<u>Vision and explanation given to Sadie Jaramillo October 13, 1999 - 1:30 p.m.</u>

(Today after Holy Mass)

JESUS: I call you to take up your pen and write the dictations of My Heart, this Heart so full of Love for my children. Yes! I am the Lion of the Tribe of Judah! Born of My Mother, I lived, died, and was resurrected, to the Glory and Praise of the Holy Trinity!

I am the Lion of the Tribe of Judah and I will win over my enemies! I will bring the hearts of all under my kingship and I will reign in the hearts of all mankind! Kings and kingdoms will be brought into my Holy Reign. The Queen of Heaven and of mankind will bring this triumphant victory swiftly to the children of God!

We have heard the cries and lamentations of all. <u>But even louder the prayers and sweet acts of adoration have risen as incense to the throne room of God.</u> The time of trial and of tribulations and sorrow has been shortened for the sake of the elect!

Describe your visions.

SJ: Since my last vision and explanation, which was received on August 1, 1999, I have been shown the following vision at various times of prayer. I see a "shower of stars" falling toward earth. This reminds me of a vision given long ago in which I saw the seven angels of the Lord hurling down to earth glowing objects like stars. I was given the understanding that these represented the destruction and catastrophic disasters that would be sent to earth for punishment and purification. My understanding is that these falling stars indicate an increase in the severity of natural disasters and in the loss of life they cause. I also believe this "shower of stars" will bring cosmic repercussions. I am not sure if they are little meteors, but they are something of that nature.

Earlier the same day, as Father J. is elevating the Body and Blood of Our Lord Jesus Christ at Mass, I see a flash of light. Then as I look upon the Host, broken in two, I see a vision of one half of the Host suddenly being thrown to the floor and a foot stomping on it to destroy it. Needless to say, this is very disturbing. I then am shown, during my thanksgiving, an image of the Sacred Heart of Jesus. From the image of His Sacred Heart comes forth a Host, again broken in two. One half is held aloft for adoration, the other half is thrown down. Again, I see a foot stomping on the Host.

Jesus (continues): The time arrives for all humanity to undergo the greatest of all trials. You will see my True Church broken in two! You will see them TRY to stamp out belief in My True Presence! This will happen as a result of the crowning title given to my mother, Mary: Co-redemptrix, Mediatrix and Advocate of all Graces! Behold! The doors open and you will see great destruction, chaos, and devastation. But you will also behold <u>great wonders of God and the greatest prodigy of Grace and Divine Mercy to transform those who will accept this grace!</u> Over and over again I call to all who would listen. Behold when the Son of Man returns to earth, do not be caught off guard! This has all been spoken of many times before. I will move the very

bowels of the earth, the rumblings of which are already being seen. There are those (people) who do not see what is known to ME. There are plans being made to bring about a planned state of chaos and confusion. But I will use these very instruments in my Justice to humble and bring all to submission.

No longer will the old, filled with wisdom, be cast aside. No longer will the cries of the innocent (those babies lost to abortion) be heard in Heaven crying for vengeance. ALL life will be held sacred for I gave this Sacred Body, Blood, Soul and Divinity to give everlasting life! The Church will be restored. There will be one flock, and there will be one shepherd. Truth will be known in all hearts, everywhere.

Hold fast to that which is placed in your heart. I will bring it about.

Persevere, my children. Be vigilant and awake! When you LEAST expect, you will feel the repercussions of my justice! I AM with you to the end! The gates of hell WILL NOT prevail! These are my promises and they are tried and true.

You, my sentinel, must tell all: "Stand firm! The shaking comes! Be ready and alert! My Grace obtained by my mother will carry you through! BE NOT AFRAID!"

SJ: : And what of C.?

JESUS: C. will rest in the bosom of her God and the Cross (of Peace) will rise to bring fulfillment of her mission. The lights of heaven will shine forth all around the world!

Be Not Afraid!

I bid you Blessings and Peace to all who believe!

SJ: Amen! Thank you Jesus.

Note to these visions and explanations:

My brothers and sisters in Christ, I greet you in the Name of the Lord Jesus Christ! As you can tell from the dates, the visions and explanations continue to come less and less frequently. I ask you all to continue to persevere, for this is a virtue that does not come easily. Keep placing one foot in front of the other, and continue a life of prayer, in spite of the attacks, in spite of the dryness, in spite of the falling away of many others who were once a part of the "remnant."

These visions indicate again, as in the many other messages, the cosmic phenomena that will accompany the Warning, or mini-judgement of our souls. I was given an understanding that the vision of doors opening concerned the opening of the Holy Door, for the Jubilee Year 2000. This door will be opened Christmas Eve by the Holy Father John Paul 11, provided that we keep praying for his strength. In this "Year of Favor" of the Lord, because of our prayers united to Jesus' Holy Cross, God will grant special graces of conversion to all those who NEED them! Many of your loved ones (and mine) will be saved by means of your faithfulness to prayer and TRUST, if only they will open their hearts to receive God's grace.

The vision of the foot stomping on the Eucharist deepens my understanding of the meaning of the Woman crushing the head of the serpent in Genesis, Chapter 3. The enemies of the Church want to stamp out our belief in the truth of the Real Presence. But that belief is what makes us uniquely Catholic. Our Lady will STAMP OUT THE CAUSE OF

THIS DIVISION, who is satan.

The desecration of the Holy Eucharist and continued apostasy in the Church continue to be the greatest signs for us that we are in the end times. The apostasy gives us all the opportunity to WITNESS to what we believe! Our Lord clearly states that there will come a split in the Church when the title of Co-redemptrix is bestowed on Our Lady, in addition to the titles of Advocate, Helper, Benefactress, and Mediatrix, under which she is presently invoked in the Church. WE CANNOT CHANGE WHAT IS HAPPENING! IT WILL HAVE TO BE DEALT WITH DIVINELY! GOD HIMSELF WILL RESTORE THE CHURCH AND THE WORLD! ALL WE HAVE TO DO IS KEEP THAT IN OUR HEARTS!

The coming Era of Peace will be the EUCHARISTIC REIGN OF JESUS AND THE TRIUMPH OF THE IMMACULATE HEART OF MARY! Mary's TRIUMPH is to bring about the Eucharistic Reign of Jesus! The more they try to stamp out our belief in the Real Presence of Jesus Christ in the Eucharist, the more God will raise up worshippers from stones to praise Him! We must give witness in a quiet way, not arguing, but firmly defending. The only way we can do that is to LEARN, LEARN, and LEARN! Read scripture, listen to apologetic tapes, videos, and LEARN THE MASS! Don't just take up space in the Mass, but PRAY the Mass. Learn the meaning of the several parts, and of the rubrics of the Mass. Holy Mother Church is the only one to whom Christ has given authority to determine how the Mass shall be celebrated, and she has provided guidelines that we, the faithful, can learn.

Most importantly, if we are receiving the Eucharist daily, receiving frequent sacramental confession, reciting the rosary each day, and attending weekly prayer cenacles, then we have nothing to fear. This is the common thread of the true messages of Our Lady and Our Lord.

I have just returned from speaking to brothers and sisters of great faith in Montana. We are not very many, but WE ARE STRONG! I find this to be true no matter where the Lord has taken me to speak. Too many people are placing dates on events and misinterpreting the messages. They want to be ready to avoid the pain, but they don't want to truly change their way of living! Most of the people I have met have undergone the "sifting" and are still persevering!

Jesus wouldn't have said, "When the Son of Man returns to the earth will He find any faith'?" if He hadn't known this would happen. (Luke 18: 8)

The final lines of the message, "…the lights of heaven will shine forth all around the world,..." refer to us here in Santa Maria, California, who have been praying that the Cross of Peace will rise to be a symbol of consolation and grace to many people. In another vision I was shown many illuminated crosses rising into the heavens. As I dared to ask the Lord a question, I was given the understanding that these illuminated crosses would rise in the heavens and the remnant would be led to these various places.

Led by Fr. Jim Anderson, we have been "storming heaven" since July. One Sunday a month we gather in Priesker Park and we pray the 15 decades of the Rosary, listen to spiritual talks and then conclude the day of prayer with a procession and Benediction of the Blessed Sacrament. We pray for all projects that are currently "under construction." Whether your project for Christ is a statue, a cross, a shrine, a prayer group, a religious community, a monastery or whatever the project, we are united with you. Please pray for us here too.

Our next day of prayer will be November 21, 1999, in honor of the feast of Christ the King. The last Sunday will be on the feast of Our Lady of Guadalupe, December 12, 1999. On that day we will also honor Our Lady under the title of the Immaculate Conception.

Please, do not be the ones Our Lady speaks about who, she says, read messages and then place them in a drawer to be forgotten. Live them! Through you, your prayers, sufferings and sacrifices, WE WILL WIN WITH OUR LADY AND JESUS!

Thank you, to all the people who pray daily for me. For those who regularly donate generously, for those who continue to be the "maintenance" workers, and for those who keep the activities going on at the House of Prayer, whether I am there or not, to all of you, THANK YOU!

Sadie Jaramillo

Be Not Afraid!

Message to Sadie Jaramillo - December 9, 1999

SJ: As I was preparing for mass I began to hear Our Lady. I began to cry because I had not "heard" anything since October 13, 1999. 1 use the word heard, but that isn't really how it is. Words fail miserably to convey the way the locution comes. But I share this part of the account because it may inspire some of you, my brothers and sisters in Christ, to persevere.

I had again been plummeted into something like "the dark night of the soul." I could find NO consolation. I would cry out to Jesus and Mary and there would be NOTHING. But since prayer and faith do not depend on my feelings, I persevered. I have also experienced, during these past weeks, persecution. Again, feeling quite disheartened, I cried out to the Lord. During one of these times I felt like I would just give in to the temptations of doubt and attacks of the evil one. Again I cried, from the depths of my heart. I heard nothing. So, with faith like a child, I said "Jesus, console my heart, I know you hear me, console my heart, for I feel I cannot go on. I know you will speak to my heart for I trust in you." I was at that point in tears, but then suddenly I was given the inspiration to get my copy of the Diary of Sister Faustina: "Divine Mercy in My Soul." I said to Jesus, "I know you will speak to me through your words to Blessed Faustina." I randomly opened the book to page 533. My eyes fell to the bold passage where Jesus speaks.

It started with Jesus saying: **"My beloved child, delight of My Heart, your words are dearer and more pleasing to me than the angelic chorus. All the treasures of My Heart are open to you. Take from this Heart all that you need for yourself and for the whole world. For the sake of your love, I withhold the just chastisements, which mankind** has deserved. A **single act of pure love pleases Me more than a thousand imperfect prayers. One of your sighs of love atones for many offenses with which the godless overwhelm Me.** The smallest act of virtue has unlimited value in My eyes because of your great love for Me. In a soul that lives on My love alone, I reign as in heaven. I watch over it day and night. In it I find My happiness; My ear is attentive to each request of its heart; often I anticipate its requests. O child, especially beloved by Me, apple of My eye, rest a moment near My Heart and taste of the love in which you will delight for all eternity.

But child, you are not yet in your homeland; so go, fortified by My grace and fight for My kingdom in human souls; fight as a king's child would; and remember that the days of your exile will pass quickly, and with them the possibility of earning merit for heaven. I expect from you, My child, a great number of souls who will glorify My mercy for all eternity. My child, that you may answer My call worthily, receive Me daily in Holy Communion, it will give you strength..."[2]

These words were enough for me. I cried all the harder, for it was as though Jesus had been there in person, talking to me.

After testing what I was hearing, Our Lady answered me in the following way:

MARY: **I, who stood at the foot of the Cross, praised the Eternal Father for the gift of His Son! I, who stood at the foot of the Cross, praised the Eternal Father that I, humble Virgin**

---

[2] <u>Diary of Blessed Sister Faustina Kowalska</u>, Third. Ed., Blessed Sister M. Faustina Kowalska, Marians of the Immaculate Conception, Stockbridge, MA, 1996, p. 533.

of Nazareth, would give birth to the Son of God: Word of God, made man by the power of the Holy Spirit! **Yes my little sorrowful rose, I praise God for Jesus' coming in the flesh!**

I have wanted to console you and through you my other children. You have been plunged into the dark night of the soul and there, persevered through the testing. You know in your heart the words of consolation given to you, and by which means it was given. (Our Lady is referring to the words described above of Sister Faustina's Diary.)

I have come to ask you to, **a little while longer, PERSEVERE.** Few are they who continue to live the messages of the heart. For that is how I have spoken, that is how I have chosen, through the Will of God, my instruments: through the heart! Each one is accomplishing through the means they have been given, the Will of God: to become transformed into little vessels of love, little victims of love. **For I am your Mother, and the Mother who saw and heard the cries of your heart. I see them still. I will NEVER abandon my children. I am here to lead my remnant to the Great Victory and Triumph of my Heart! And what is this Triumph: that ALL will know the EUCHARISTIC LORD! In this victory ALL enemies of this Truth will be brought low!**

In this (coming) year of (God's) favor, in this year of great blessings, in this year that brings three preparatory years of Mercy to a close, you will cross the great Threshold of Hope and Joy into the (next) millennium where God will place ALL enemies under His feet. I will lead and protect my army to a great (spiritual) Victory! This Victory will allow all hearts to reconcile themselves to their creator!

What you have labored for, what you have suffered for, you will only see in the Glory of heaven! (Here Our Lady refers to those of us who have responded to the requests of Jesus and Mary to pray and be willing to suffer for souls.) **Souls will see and rejoice in the Great Light! Souls will see and be brought forth from darkness. Souls will see in the fullness of TRUTH the Great Mercy of God!**

I wish to encourage you and all in this time of rejoicing! Those prepared on the Rock (faith in Jesus and his holy Church) will triumph with me!

My Son has already announced to you the great catastrophes that will befall this humanity. The earth will shake, for the justice of God; kingdoms will fall, for the justice of God; idols will be destroyed, for the justice of God; nations plotting destruction will be crushed, for the justice of God; the enemies of Christ will be destroyed, for the JUSTICE OF GOD IS A MIGHTY THING!

The scales will soon turn and my Triumph will be seen in a more forceful way by those with eyes to see and ears to hear.

I, the Queen of Heaven and the Mother of this humanity come to ask you to Rejoice, 0 little ones of God! In this year of favor will be seen the Great Light, REJOICE!

I bless and hold you and all who believe in My Immaculate Heart!

SJ: AMEN!

THE GREAT SIGN
VOL. I & VOL. II
Messages and Visions of Final Warnings

Powerful books on God's warnings and great mercy to prepare us, His children for a new Era of Peace. His greatest act of mercy will be a universal warning or illumination of souls, accompanied by a miraculous luminous cross in a dark sky.

You must read these books if you want to learn how:

✝ The Mother of All Humanity warns her children.
✝ Priests must inform and prepare God's people, with faith, hope, love, prayer and sacrifice.
✝ The thunder of God's justice will resound and nature will mirror the fury of God's anger, bringing mankind to its knees.
✝ Worldwide economic and financial collapse will far surpass anything that has ever happened.
✝ The Church and the Pope will be attacked.
✝ **The GREAT SIGN, a miraculous, luminous cross in the sky**, will accompany **the warning or illumination of souls.**
✝ Forces of Antichrist will impose worldwide order and the sign of the beast.
✝ The Holy Rosary is a most powerful weapon to strengthen and protect.
✝ Christ will end the rebellion and bring a glorious, new Era of Peace for His Father's remnant which remains true.

Order Form

❑ **Yes**, I would like to receive:
❑ **THE GREAT SIGN** for **$14.95**, plus **$4.95** shipping and handling.
❑ **THE GREAT SIGN VOL.II** for **$9.95**, plus **$3.95** shipping and handling.
 Canada add $5 additional for each book shipping and handling.
 Please call if ordering both or multiples copies for shipping charges,
 and foreign shipping rates. (VA residents add 4.5% sales tax.)

❑ Check or Money Order enclosed. U.S. funds only.

❑ MasterCard ❑ VISA ❑ Discover   Expiration Date _____

Card# ☐☐☐☐☐☐☐☐☐☐☐☐☐☐☐☐ (Include all 13 or 16 digits)

Signature (required for credit card orders) _____

Name/Recipient _____
Address _____
City _____ State _____ Zip _____
Work (____) _____ Home (____) _____

Please make checks to **SIGNS AND WONDERS** for Our Times
PO Box 345, Herndon, VA 20172-0345.
Call our Order Department at (703) 327-2277 or FAX (703) 327-2888

Heaven's Messages for The Family
Volumes I & II
NEW

How to become the family God wants you to be.

"The future of humanity passes by way of the family"
—*Pope John Paul II*

Families are under attack by the forces of evil. The rise in divorce, spousal violence and child abuse - all point to a situation which makes supernatural intervention appropriate and credible.

Mrs. Janie Garza of Austin, Texas, wife, mother and mystic was chosen by the Lord to be a vessel of simple and holy messages for the family of today. She has been receiving messages and visions since February 15, 1989, up to the present time.

Read and learn about:

☦ What the main spiritual attacks are against the family today.

☦ The spiritual tools given by Heaven to combat the attacks against the family.

☦ What the roles of the husband, wife and children are according to God's divine order.

☦ What you can do to protect your marriage and family members.

☦ The seven visions about the state of the world and families today.

☦ How prayer in each family is the spiritual pre-condition for world peace and the renewal of the universal Church.

This divinely-inspired book is a comprehensive manual of spiritual guidance for today's families! Heaven shows us the tools to be holy. Guaranteed to bring you and your family closer to God and to each other.
—*Ted and Maureen Flynn*
Co-authors of <u>THE THUNDER OF JUSTICE</u>

Order Now at the Special Publication Price of only $14.95 each
-plus $3.95 shipping and handling for each book.

Canada add $5.00 additional for each book shipping and handling.

(VA residents add 4.5% sales tax)

ST. DOMINIC MEDIA
Phone: 703-327-2277 Fax: 703-327-2888
P.O. Box 345 • Herndon, Virginia • 20172-0345

Warnings, Visions & Messages

Father Hebert has written another
BLOCKBUSTER!

A comprehensive overview of the visions, messages and warnings given to various Irish visionaries today about the times we are in; warnings, visions, and messages for the entire world.

Our Lord and his Blessed Mother are warning Mankind before Chastisement disasters strike.

The famous "Our Lady of Knock" silent apparitions of 1879 that opened the Apocalyptic Times blend today with new apparitions, urgent messages and merciful warnings of a Great Chastisement, if the warnings are not heeded.

READ AND LEARN ABOUT:

- *Miraculous phenomena and movements of statues documented on video.*
- *Irish children witnessing biblical visions and warnings of impending judgment if Mankind does not repent.*
- *Christine Gallagher, one of the greatest mystics, stigmatists and visionaries of our times; visionaries Beulah Lynch and Mark Trainer from Bessbrook, Ireland receive Apocalyptic visions and messages of great disasters.*
- *Visions of the Great Era of Peace*

Book Order Form

☐ Yes, I would like to receive **Warnings, Visions & Messages**. Please send me _____ copies for **$9.95, plus $2.95** shipping and handling within the **United States**. Please call for exact **foreign** shipping rates. **Canada - Add $5.00** additional for each book-shipping and handling.

☐ Check or Money Order enclosed. U.S. funds only

☐ MasterCard ☐ VISA ☐ Discover   Expiration Date _____

Card # ☐☐☐☐☐☐☐☐☐☐☐☐☐☐☐☐ (Include all 13 or 16 digits)

Signature *(required for credit card orders)* _____

Name/Recipient _____

Address _____

City _____ State _____ Zip _____

Work ( ) _____ Home ( ) _____

Please make checks to SIGNS AND WONDERS for Our Times • P.O. Box 345, Herndon, VA 20172-0345. For immediate attention, call our Order Department at (703) 327-2277 or FAX (703) 327-2888

Tribulations and Triumph

The End of An Evil Era and the Dawn of a New Glorious Time...

Now, a new voice from the American Midwest is added to the Chorus. The Lord is giving an American housewife, Joanne Kriva, words of warning and pleas for peace—and imparting details of events that will soon overtake the world. Joanne's new volume focuses on the messages she received from Our Lord and Lady between February 1995 to August 1996.

Read and Learn:
- why the apparitions of Our Lady are about to close;
- the dangers that threaten Pope John Paul II—and his place within the Divine Providence;
- how the Antichrist is alive and plotting to fully exert his power in the world;
- how destruction will be unleashed on a scale never before witnessed in human history;
- what glorious era awaits those who remain faithful during these troubled times.

Book Order Form

☐ Yes, I would like to receive *Tribulations and Triumph!* Volume 2 for $6.95, plus $2.95 shipping and handling for the first copy and $1.00 for each additional copy sent within the US. Canada add $5.00 additional for each book shipping and handling. Please call for exact foreign shipping rates..

☐ Check or Money Order enclosed. U.S. funds only

☐ MasterCard ☐ VISA ☐ Discover   Expiration Date _____

Card # ☐☐☐☐☐☐☐☐☐☐☐☐☐☐☐☐ (Include all 13 or 16 digits)

Signature *(required for credit card orders)* _____

My Name/Recipient _____

Address _____

City _____ State _____ Zip _____

Work ( ) _____ Home ( ) _____

Please make checks to SIGNS AND WONDERS for Our Times • P.O. Box 345, Herndon, VA 20172-0345. For immediate attention, call our Order Department at (703) 327-2277 or FAX (703) 327-2888

Earthquakes. Abortion. Crime. Family Breakdown. Corruption. War.

Signs and Wonders
for our Times

We, at *Signs and Wonders for Our Times* Catholic magazine, know that heaven is intervening in a powerful way. In these end times, our Blessed Mother has come from Heaven with messages for the whole world—revealing secrets of the future and calling for peace.

With the dramatic increase in apparitions occurring on all continents like never before, *Signs and Wonders for Our Times* exists to provide access to some of the most important information of our age. With the latest messages and visits from heaven, timely features interpreting the *signs of our times, miraculous healing and conversion stories, church history and devotions,* the all-new children's corner—each issue promises to enrich you spiritually and prepare you for what lies ahead. Be part of Our Lady's army and equip yourself

---

Subscription Request Form

☐ Yes, sign me up now for a 1 year subscription (four quarterly issues) to *Signs and Wonders for Our Times*. I understand the price is $24 per year for U.S. subscriptions; $36 to Canada; $60 to all other foreign countries.
U.S. Funds Only.

☐ Check or Money Order enclosed. U.S. funds only

☐ MasterCard ☐ VISA ☐ Discover   Expiration Date _____

Card # ☐☐☐☐☐☐☐☐☐☐☐☐☐☐☐☐   (Include all 13 or 16 digits)

Signature *(required for credit card orders)* _____

My Name/Recipient _____

Address _____

City _____ State _____ Zip _____

Work ( ) _____ Home ( ) _____

Phone number is required to process order.

Please make checks to SIGNS AND WONDERS for Our Times • P.O. Box 345, Herndon, VA 20172-0345. For immediate attention, call our Order Department at (703) 327-2277 or FAX (703) 327-2888 Thank you for your love and support.

Read Tomorrow's News TODAY!

Subscribe to
Catholic Prophecy Update

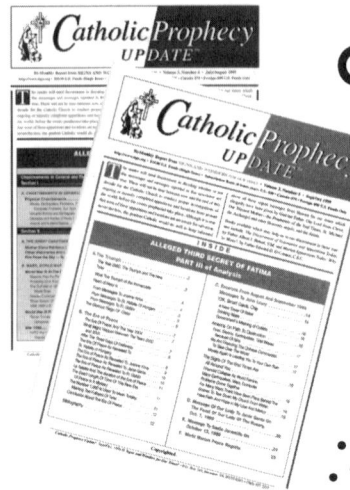

Bimonthly reports on:
- The Warning / The Miracle
- The Mark of the Beast
- The Smart Card and the Microchip
- The Fate of Pope John Paul II
- The Great Tribulation
- The Persecution of the true Church
- The Antichrist and One World Government
- Natural Disasters and the Comets
- The New Era of Peace, And MORE!

ORDER FORM   *Choose one of the following:*

☐ **YES, I want to become a *Catholic Prophecy Partner*.** Here is my annual membership of $50.00 and I will receive the *Catholic Prophecy Update* bimonthly. My donation is included in this.

☐ **YES, please give a GIFT SUBSCRIPTION to *Catholic Prophecy Update*.**
   ☐ U.S.-$50 ☐ Canada-$70 ☐ Foreign-$100

   Please send the name, address, telephone, (if applicable) of both sender and recipient.

☐ **YES, I would like to become a monthly partner for the *Triumph of the Two Hearts*.** Here is my monthly donation:
   ☐ $10 ☐ $20 ☐ $25 ☐ $50 ☐ $100
   ☐ other

☐ **YES, I would like the 1997 *Catholic Prophecy Update* Binder** - 6 issues in one place for **$49.95** including shipping and handling.

   Topics include: the Warning, the Miracle, the Mark of the Beast, the SMART card, the Great Apostasy, the Antichrist and the Triumph.

☐ Check or Money Order. U.S. funds only   Signature _____

☐ MasterCard   ☐ VISA   ☐ Discover   Expiration Date _____

Card # ☐☐☐☐☐☐☐☐☐☐☐☐☐☐☐☐   (Include entire number, 13 or 16 digits)

My Name/Donor _____

Address _____

City _____ State _____ Zip _____

Work ( ) _____ Home ( ) _____

FAX # ( ) _____ (if this subscription will be received by fax)

Please make checks to SIGNS AND WONDERS for Our Times
P.O. Box 345, Herndon, VA 20172-0345.
For immediate attention, Call (703) 327-2277 or FAX (703) 327-2888